Table Of Contents

Chapter 1: Introduction to Domain Flipping

Understanding Domain Flipping

Domain flipping is a lucrative business opportunity that has gained significant popularity in recent years. It involves buying and selling domain names for profit, and it offers several avenues for entrepreneurs, students, fresh graduates, young entrepreneurs, and even parents to make money online. In this subchapter, we will explore the various aspects of domain flipping and how individuals can tap into this market to flip their fortunes.

One of the primary ways to make money from domain names is through domain flipping. This strategy involves purchasing valuable domain names at a low price and selling them at a higher price. By identifying trends, popular keywords, or potential future demand, domain flippers can acquire domains that are likely to appreciate in value over time. This niche of domain flipping requires research, knowledge of market trends, and a keen eye for identifying valuable domain names.

Another option for generating income from domain names is domain parking. This involves displaying ads on unused domain names to earn money through pay-per-click advertising. By parking a domain, entrepreneurs can monetize their unused domains and earn passive income without having to develop a website or online business.

Domain brokerage is another avenue for entrepreneurs to explore. Acting as a middleman, domain brokers connect buyers and sellers of domain names and earn a commission for facilitating the transaction. This niche requires negotiation skills, market knowledge, and a strong network within the domain industry.

Domain investing involves building a portfolio of valuable domain names and earning income through their appreciation over time. This strategy requires a long-term perspective and understanding of the market to identify domains with potential value. Domain investors can also explore domain development, creating websites or online businesses on purchased domain names to generate revenue through advertising, e-commerce, or other monetization methods.

Other ways to profit from domain names include offering domain registration services, domain appraisal services, domain consulting, participating in domain auctions, and optimizing and monetizing existing websites or blogs with valuable domain names.

In conclusion, domain flipping offers a range of opportunities for entrepreneurs, students, fresh graduates, young entrepreneurs, and even parents to make money online. With the right knowledge, research, and strategy, individuals can tap into the various niches of domain flipping and flip their fortunes in the ever-expanding domain market. Whether it is buying and selling domain names, parking unused domains, acting as a domain broker, or investing in valuable domain names, domain flipping has the potential to be a profitable venture for those willing to put in the effort and stay ahead of the curve in this fast-paced industry.

The Potential of Domain Flipping

In the ever-evolving world of online entrepreneurship, domain flipping has emerged as a lucrative opportunity for those looking to make money from the comfort of their own homes. This subchapter explores the vast potential of domain flipping and its various niches, providing valuable insights and strategies for entrepreneurs, students, fresh graduates, young entrepreneurs, and even parents.

Domain flipping, also known as buying and selling domain names for profit, offers a range of opportunities for individuals to generate income. The first niche, domain parking, involves earning money by displaying ads on unused domain names. By simply registering a domain and parking it with a reputable service, entrepreneurs can earn passive income through ad clicks and impressions.

Another niche, domain brokerage, involves acting as a middleman to connect domain buyers and sellers for a commission. With the right negotiation skills and knowledge of the market, entrepreneurs can facilitate lucrative deals and earn a substantial income in the process.

Domain investing, on the other hand, focuses on building a portfolio of valuable domain names and earning income through their appreciation. By identifying trending keywords and purchasing domain names that align with popular niches, entrepreneurs can capitalize on the growing demand for online real estate.

For those with a knack for creativity, domain development offers a unique avenue to generate revenue. By creating websites or online businesses on purchased domain names, entrepreneurs can leverage their skills to attract visitors and monetize their online platforms.

Additionally, domain monetization involves optimizing and monetizing existing websites or blogs with valuable domain names. Through various strategies such as affiliate marketing, sponsored content, and ad placements, entrepreneurs can turn their online presence into a profitable venture.

Furthermore, entrepreneurs can explore the niche of domain registration services, offering domain registration services and earning income through registration fees. By providing a seamless and efficient service, entrepreneurs can establish themselves as trusted domain registrars in a competitive market.

Domain appraisal is another niche that entrepreneurs can explore, providing domain appraisal services to determine the value of domain names for buyers and sellers. By leveraging their expertise and knowledge of the market, entrepreneurs can assist individuals or businesses in making informed decisions regarding domain name strategies.

Lastly, domain auctions present an opportunity for entrepreneurs to participate in and profit from online domain auctions by buying and selling domain names. By staying updated on the latest trends and conducting thorough research, entrepreneurs can secure valuable domains at auctions and sell them at a profit.

In conclusion, the potential of domain flipping is vast and varied. From domain parking and brokerage to investing, development, and monetization, there are numerous avenues for entrepreneurs, students, fresh graduates, young entrepreneurs, and even parents to explore and capitalize on. By harnessing the power of domain names, individuals can carve out a profitable niche in the online landscape.

Benefits and Challenges of Domain Flipping

Domain flipping, the practice of buying and selling domain names for profit, has gained significant popularity in recent years. This subchapter explores the benefits and challenges that come with this lucrative venture.

For entrepreneurs, domain flipping offers a unique opportunity to make money from domain names. With the right strategy and market knowledge, one can buy undervalued domain names and sell them at a higher price, earning a substantial profit. This can be an attractive income stream for students, fresh graduates, and young entrepreneurs looking to make extra money or start their own online business.

One of the main benefits of domain flipping is the potential for high returns. A well-researched and targeted domain name can fetch thousands or even millions of dollars when sold to the right buyer. This can be an appealing prospect for individuals looking to invest in a profitable venture.

Domain flipping also allows individuals to tap into various niches within the domain industry. Whether it's domain parking, brokerage, investing, development, or monetization, there are multiple avenues to explore based on one's interests and expertise. This versatility ensures that entrepreneurs can find the niche that aligns with their skills and goals.

However, along with the benefits, there are also challenges associated with domain flipping. The first challenge is identifying valuable domain names. With millions of domains already registered, finding the right domain that holds potential for future appreciation can be a daunting task. It requires extensive research, market analysis, and a keen eye for emerging trends.

Another challenge is the competitive nature of the domain flipping industry. Many experienced domain flippers are constantly on the lookout for profitable opportunities, making it crucial for newcomers to stay ahead of the game. Building a strong network and staying updated with industry trends and market demand is vital to succeed in this fast-paced environment.

Lastly, domain flipping requires patience and persistence. It may take months or even years to find the right buyer for a domain and realize a significant profit. It is crucial to have a long-term mindset and be prepared for the ups and downs that come with this business.

In conclusion, domain flipping offers numerous benefits for entrepreneurs, students, fresh graduates, and young entrepreneurs looking to make money online. It provides opportunities to explore various niches within the domain industry and earn substantial profits. However, it also comes with challenges, such as identifying valuable domain names and dealing with competition. With the right knowledge, strategy, and perseverance, domain flipping can be a rewarding venture for those willing to put in the effort.

Essential Skills for Successful Domain Flipping

In the ever-evolving world of online entrepreneurship, domain flipping has emerged as a lucrative and exciting opportunity for individuals looking to make money from the comfort of their own homes. Whether you are an entrepreneur, student, fresh graduate, young entrepreneur, or even a parent seeking an additional source of income, mastering the art of domain flipping can help you achieve your financial goals.

Domain flipping involves buying and selling domain names for profit. It encompasses various niches, such as domain parking, brokerage, investing, development, monetization, registration services, appraisal, consulting, and auctions. Regardless of the niche you choose, there are several essential skills you must possess to succeed in this field.

First and foremost, research is the backbone of successful domain flipping. You need to stay up-to-date with the latest trends and market demands. Conduct comprehensive market research to identify valuable domain names that have the potential to generate a high return on investment. Utilize tools and platforms that provide insights into domain name popularity, search engine optimization, and market value.

Next, negotiation skills are crucial when it comes to domain flipping. As a middleman connecting buyers and sellers, or when participating in auctions, it is essential to negotiate the best deals on behalf of your clients or yourself. Be confident, persuasive, and know the value of the domain name you are offering or seeking.

Furthermore, marketing and branding skills play a significant role in successful domain flipping. You need to understand how to create a compelling online presence for your domain names, whether it is through developing websites or optimizing existing ones. Effective marketing strategies will help attract potential buyers and increase the value of your domain names.

In addition, financial management skills are essential to ensure profitability in domain flipping. Keep track of your investments, expenses, and revenue to make informed decisions. Budget wisely and reinvest your profits strategically to grow your portfolio and maximize your earning potential.

Lastly, networking and building relationships within the domain flipping community are essential for success. Attend industry conferences, join online forums, and connect with other domain flippers to gain knowledge, share experiences, and access potential buyers and sellers.

Mastering these essential skills will empower you to thrive in the world of domain flipping. Whether you choose to specialize in domain parking, brokerage, investing, development, monetization, registration services, appraisal, consulting, or auctions, these skills will be your foundation for a successful and profitable venture. Embrace the art of domain flipping, and unlock the door to financial freedom.

Chapter 2: Getting Started with Domain Flipping

Researching and Selecting Profitable Domain Names

In the digital era, domain names have become valuable assets for individuals and businesses alike. They hold the power to create online identities, drive traffic, and generate substantial profits. As an entrepreneur, student, fresh graduate, young entrepreneur, or parent, understanding the art of domain flipping can open up a world of opportunities to make money from domain names.

Domain flipping involves buying and selling domain names for profit. It is a lucrative niche that offers multiple avenues for income generation. One such avenue is domain parking, where unused domain names are monetized by displaying ads. By leveraging the traffic potential of these domains, entrepreneurs can earn passive income.

Another profitable domain flipping strategy is domain brokerage. Acting as a middleman, you connect buyers and sellers and earn a commission for facilitating the transaction. This requires strong negotiation skills and an in-depth understanding of the domain market.

Domain investing involves building a portfolio of valuable domain names and earning income through their appreciation. This strategy requires meticulous research and analysis to identify undervalued domains that have the potential to increase in value over time.

For those with a flair for creativity, domain development presents an exciting opportunity. By creating websites or online businesses on purchased domain names, entrepreneurs can generate revenue through various monetization methods such as advertising, affiliate marketing, or e-commerce.

Domain monetization, on the other hand, focuses on optimizing and monetizing existing websites or blogs with valuable domain names. By strategically placing ads and leveraging affiliate partnerships, entrepreneurs can maximize their earnings potential.

Entrepreneurs looking to enter the domain industry may consider offering domain registration services. By becoming a registrar and charging registration fees, they can create a sustainable income stream.

Additionally, providing domain appraisal services can be a profitable venture. By determining the value of domain names for buyers and sellers, entrepreneurs can offer expert advice and guidance, ensuring fair transactions.

Participating in domain auctions is another avenue to profit from domain flipping. By meticulously researching and acquiring valuable domain names, entrepreneurs can sell them for a significant profit.

Whether you are an aspiring entrepreneur, a student, a fresh graduate, a young entrepreneur, or a parent looking to diversify your income streams, researching and selecting profitable domain names is a skill worth mastering. It offers a range of niches within the domain industry, each with its unique income potential. With dedication, research, and a keen eye for valuable domains, you can flip your fortune and unlock the hidden potential of domain flipping.

Registering and Acquiring Domain Names

In the world of online entrepreneurship, one of the most crucial steps to success is registering and acquiring domain names. Whether you are an experienced entrepreneur, a student looking for a side hustle, a fresh graduate eager to make a mark, a young entrepreneur starting out, or even a parent seeking additional income, understanding the art of domain flipping can be a game-changer.

Domain flipping refers to the practice of buying and selling domain names for profit. It is a lucrative business that can be pursued in various ways. One popular method is domain parking, where you earn money by displaying ads on unused domain names. By leveraging the traffic potential of these domains, you can generate passive income.

Another approach is domain brokerage, acting as a middleman to connect domain buyers and sellers for a commission. This requires a keen eye for identifying valuable domain names and a knack for negotiation. Domain investing, on the other hand, involves building a portfolio of valuable domain names and earning income through their appreciation over time.

If you have a flair for creativity, domain development might be your calling. With this strategy, you create websites or online businesses on purchased domain names to generate revenue. By offering valuable content or products, you can attract visitors and monetize your website effectively.

Domain monetization focuses on optimizing and monetizing existing websites or blogs with valuable domain names. By implementing advertising networks, affiliate marketing, or selling digital products, you can maximize the profitability of your online assets.

If you have a passion for helping others, domain consulting might be your niche. Offering expert advice and guidance on domain name strategies can be a valuable service to individuals or businesses looking to establish a strong online presence.

For those who prefer a more hands-on approach, domain auctions provide a thrilling opportunity to participate and profit from online domain auctions. By strategically buying and selling domain names, you can capitalize on market trends and make a significant return on investment.

In conclusion, registering and acquiring domain names offer a plethora of opportunities to make money online. Whether you choose to specialize in domain flipping, domain parking, domain brokerage, domain investing, domain development, domain monetization, domain registration services, domain appraisal, domain consulting, or domain auctions, the potential for financial success is immense. So, take the plunge and explore the exciting world of domain flipping, where your entrepreneurial dreams can become a reality.

Evaluating the Value of Domain Names

In the fast-paced digital era, domain names have become valuable assets that can be leveraged to generate substantial income. Whether you are an entrepreneur, student, fresh graduate, young entrepreneur, or even a parent looking for new avenues of income, understanding the value of domain names is essential. This subchapter will delve into the various aspects of evaluating the worth of domain names, empowering you to make informed decisions in the dynamic world of domain flipping.

Domain flipping, the art of buying and selling domain names for profit, has emerged as a lucrative business opportunity. To succeed in this field, it is crucial to assess the value of domain names accurately. A domain name's value is determined by several factors, including its length, keyword relevance, brandability, and potential for generating organic traffic. Furthermore, considering market trends, industry demand, and the target audience's preferences can significantly impact a domain's value.

Domain parking, domain brokerage, domain investing, and domain development are among the diverse avenues for monetizing domain names. Each strategy requires a distinct evaluation approach. For instance, domain parking focuses on earning money by displaying ads on unused domain names. In this case, factors like ad click-through rates, niche relevance, and the potential for attracting advertisers become crucial determinants of a domain's value.

Additionally, domain monetization involves optimizing and monetizing existing websites or blogs with valuable domain names. Here, factors like website traffic, quality content, and potential revenue streams play a pivotal role in assessing a domain's worth.

To accurately evaluate a domain name's value, domain appraisal services can be sought. These services provide expert insights into the market value of a domain, considering factors such as domain age, search engine optimization metrics, and historical sales data. Domain appraisal services are invaluable tools for both buyers and sellers, ensuring fair transactions and maximizing profits.

Furthermore, domain consulting can provide individuals or businesses with expert advice on domain name strategies. These consultants specialize in identifying trends, analyzing market demand, and utilizing domain names to their maximum potential. By seeking guidance from domain consultants, you can gain a competitive edge and make well-informed decisions.

Lastly, participating in domain auctions is another avenue for buying and selling domain names. Online domain auctions provide a platform for entrepreneurs to showcase their domain names and attract potential buyers. By understanding market trends, valuing domain names accurately, and strategically bidding, domain auctions can be highly profitable.

In conclusion, evaluating the value of domain names is crucial for anyone looking to dive into the world of domain flipping. By considering factors such as keyword relevance, market trends, and potential revenue streams, you can make informed decisions and maximize your profits. Whether through domain parking, development, investing, or other strategies, understanding the worth of domain names will enable you to unlock the true potential of this thriving industry.

Setting Realistic Goals and Expectations

In the fast-paced world of domain flipping, it is essential to set realistic goals and expectations to ensure long-term success. Whether you are an entrepreneur, student, fresh graduate, young entrepreneur, or a parent looking to make some extra income, understanding the various niches within the domain flipping industry is crucial.

One of the most popular ways to make money from domain names is through domain flipping. This involves buying and selling domain names for profit. However, it is important to set realistic goals when starting out. It may take time and effort to find valuable domain names and build your reputation in the industry. Setting achievable targets for the number of domains you buy and sell each month can help you stay motivated and focused.

Domain parking is another avenue to earn money by displaying ads on unused domain names. While it may seem like a passive income stream, it is important to manage your expectations. The income generated from domain parking can vary greatly depending on the quality of the domain and the amount of traffic it receives. Understanding this will help you set realistic goals for your potential earnings.

If you have excellent negotiation skills, domain brokerage may be a suitable niche for you. Acting as a middleman to connect domain buyers and sellers for a commission requires building relationships and trust with both parties involved. Setting realistic expectations for the number of successful transactions you can facilitate in a given time frame can help you measure your progress and success.

Domain investing involves building a portfolio of valuable domain names and earning income through their appreciation. However, it is important to recognize that domain values can fluctuate, and it may take time for your investments to yield significant returns. Setting realistic expectations for the growth of your portfolio and being patient with your investments can lead to long-term success.

Domain development and monetization are other options to generate revenue from purchased domain names. However, it is important to understand the time and effort required to create successful websites or online businesses. Setting realistic goals for the number of websites you can develop and the revenue you expect to generate will help you stay focused and motivated.

Other niches within the domain flipping industry, such as domain registration services, domain appraisal, domain consulting, and domain auctions, also require careful goal-setting and expectation management. Understanding the potential income streams and challenges associated with each niche will help you set achievable goals and measure your progress.

In conclusion, setting realistic goals and expectations is vital in the world of domain flipping. Whether you are looking to make money from domain names, become a domain broker, or engage in any other niche within the industry, having a clear understanding of the potential challenges and rewards will help you set achievable targets and measure your success.

Chapter 3: Make Money From Domain Names

Monetizing Domain Names through Advertising

In the digital age, domain names have become virtual real estate, and savvy entrepreneurs are finding innovative ways to monetize their valuable assets. By tapping into the power of advertising, individuals can transform their unused or underutilized domain names into profitable revenue streams. In this subchapter, we will explore various strategies to monetize domain names through advertising, providing you with the knowledge and tools to maximize your earning potential.

One popular method of generating income from domain names is through domain parking. Essentially, this involves displaying targeted advertisements on unused domain names, allowing you to earn money every time a visitor clicks on an ad. With the right domain parking platform, you can optimize your earnings by displaying relevant ads that resonate with your target audience.

Another avenue to explore is domain development. By creating websites or online businesses on purchased domain names, you can generate revenue through advertising. By creating compelling content and attracting a steady stream of traffic, you can attract advertisers who are willing to pay to display their ads on your platform. With careful planning and strategic execution, domain development can be a lucrative way to monetize your domain names.

For those with a knack for negotiation and connecting people, domain brokerage offers a promising opportunity. Acting as a middleman, you can earn a commission by connecting domain buyers and sellers. By leveraging your expertise and industry knowledge, you can facilitate profitable transactions and earn a handsome income in the process.

Domain investing is another option to consider. By building a portfolio of valuable domain names, you can earn income through their appreciation. As the demand for domain names continues to rise, strategic investments can yield substantial returns in the long run.

Additionally, domain monetization involves optimizing and monetizing existing websites or blogs with valuable domain names. By implementing effective advertising strategies, such as pay-per-click or affiliate marketing, you can turn your website into a profitable venture.

Other avenues to explore include offering domain registration services, providing domain appraisal services, offering expert domain consulting, and participating in domain auctions. Each of these niches presents unique opportunities to monetize domain names through advertising, allowing you to capitalize on the growing digital market.

Whether you are an entrepreneur, student, fresh graduate, young entrepreneur, or a parent looking for additional income, monetizing domain names through advertising offers a flexible and scalable opportunity. With the right strategies and mindset, you can turn your domain names into valuable assets that generate passive income and pave the way for financial success.

Affiliate Marketing with Domain Names

In the world of domain flipping, there are numerous ways to turn a profit and make your mark in the online marketplace. One such method is through affiliate marketing with domain names. This subchapter will explore the exciting possibilities of combining affiliate marketing with the lucrative world of domain flipping.

Affiliate marketing involves promoting products or services on behalf of a company and earning a commission for every sale or lead generated through your efforts. By strategically aligning domain names with relevant affiliate programs, you can create a powerful income stream that can yield substantial financial rewards.

For entrepreneurs, students, fresh graduates, young entrepreneurs, and even parents looking to make money from domain names, affiliate marketing provides a flexible and scalable business model. It allows you to leverage your domain assets to generate passive income while tapping into the vast potential of affiliate partnerships.

Domain flipping and affiliate marketing go hand in hand. By acquiring domain names that are highly relevant to popular products or services, you can create a targeted marketing platform. When visitors land on your domain, you can seamlessly integrate affiliate links or banners that direct them to relevant offers. With each conversion, you earn a commission, maximizing the potential of your domain investment.

The key to successful affiliate marketing with domain names lies in careful research and selection. Understanding your target audience, their needs, and the products or services they are likely to be interested in is crucial. By aligning your domain names with affiliate programs that cater to these specific interests, you increase the likelihood of conversions and, consequently, your earnings.

Additionally, it is essential to optimize your domain names and accompanying websites for search engines. By implementing effective SEO strategies and creating valuable, engaging content, you can drive organic traffic to your domains, increasing the chances of affiliate conversions.

Affiliate marketing with domain names offers a multitude of opportunities for enterprising individuals. Whether you choose to focus on specific niches or adopt a more diverse approach, the potential for success is vast. By combining the art of domain flipping with the power of affiliate marketing, you can unlock the true potential of your domain investments and create a lucrative online business.

So, whether you're looking to make money from domain names, engage in domain flipping, or explore various domain-related avenues such as domain parking, domain brokerage, or domain investing, affiliate marketing can amplify your earnings and propel you towards financial success. With careful planning, strategic partnerships, and diligent execution, you can turn your domain names into money-making machines and secure your place in the ever-evolving world of online entrepreneurship.

Utilizing Dropshipping with Domain Names

In the world of domain flipping, there is a lucrative opportunity that many entrepreneurs, students, fresh graduates, young entrepreneurs, and even parents can take advantage of - utilizing dropshipping with domain names. This innovative strategy allows individuals to build successful online businesses without the need for inventory or shipping hassles.

Dropshipping is a business model where you act as the middleman between suppliers and customers. Instead of purchasing products upfront and storing them in a warehouse, you simply list the products on your website or online marketplace and when a customer makes a purchase, you forward the order to the supplier who then ships the products directly to the customer. It's a win-win situation where you earn a profit without the hassle of inventory management.

When combined with domain flipping, dropshipping becomes an even more powerful tool. Here's how it works:

First, you identify high-demand niche markets or trending products that have the potential for profitability. Conduct thorough market research to understand the target audience, competition, and pricing trends.

Next, utilize your domain flipping skills to find and secure domain names relevant to the niche or product you've chosen. A memorable and keyword-rich domain name can attract more visitors and increase the perceived value of your online store.

Once you have your domain name, set up a professional-looking website or e-commerce store. Choose a reliable dropshipping platform that integrates seamlessly with your website and allows you to easily import and manage product listings.

Now it's time to find reputable suppliers who offer the products you want to sell. Look for suppliers with competitive pricing, quality products, and reliable shipping services. Establish partnerships with them and negotiate favorable terms.

With your website up and running, it's time to start marketing your online store. Utilize various digital marketing strategies such as search engine optimization, social media marketing, content marketing, and email marketing to drive traffic to your website.

As orders start pouring in, focus on providing excellent customer service and ensuring timely delivery of products. Keep a close eye on your inventory and restock products as needed to avoid any delays or backorders.

By combining the power of dropshipping and domain flipping, you can create a profitable online business without the need for significant upfront investment or inventory management. This strategy allows you to tap into the growing e-commerce industry and earn a steady income.

So, whether you're an entrepreneur looking for a new venture, a student or fresh graduate searching for a side hustle, or a young entrepreneur aiming to make a mark in the online business world, utilizing dropshipping with domain names is a smart and viable option. Don't miss out on this opportunity to flip your fortune and achieve financial success. Start exploring the world of dropshipping with domain names today!

Creating and Selling Digital Products on Domain Names

In the digital age, domain names have become valuable assets that can be bought, sold, and monetized for profit. If you're an entrepreneur, student, fresh graduate, young entrepreneur, or even a parent looking to make some extra income, the world of domain flipping and digital product creation awaits you.

Make Money From Domain Names:

One of the most popular ways to generate income from domain names is through domain flipping. This involves buying undervalued domain names and reselling them at a higher price. With the right research and marketing strategies, you can turn a small investment into a substantial profit.

Domain Parking:

If you own unused domain names, you can earn money by displaying ads on them. This is known as domain parking and can be a passive income stream. By optimizing your parked domains and driving traffic to them, you can increase the chances of ad clicks and revenue generation.

Domain Brokerage:

Acting as a middleman to connect domain buyers and sellers for a commission can be a lucrative business. As a domain broker, you can leverage your knowledge and network to facilitate domain transactions and earn a percentage of the sales.

Domain Investing:

Building a portfolio of valuable domain names and earning income through their appreciation is another profitable avenue. By identifying market trends and investing in high-demand domain names, you can benefit from their increasing value over time.

Domain Development:

Creating websites or online businesses on purchased domain names is a great way to generate revenue. By utilizing digital marketing strategies and offering valuable content or products, you can attract visitors and monetize your online platform through various channels such as advertising, affiliate marketing, or selling digital products.

Domain Monetization:

If you already own websites or blogs with valuable domain names, you can optimize and monetize them further. This can be done by implementing effective SEO strategies, partnering with advertisers, or offering premium content or services.

Domain Registration Services:

Offering domain registration services can provide a steady income through registration fees. By providing a user-friendly platform and excellent customer service, you can attract individuals and businesses looking to secure their online presence.

Domain Appraisal:

Providing domain appraisal services is a valuable niche in the domain industry. By offering expert evaluations to determine the value of domain names, you can assist buyers and sellers in making informed decisions and charge a fee for your expertise.

Domain Consulting:

If you have extensive knowledge and experience in domain name strategies, you can offer expert advice and guidance to individuals or businesses. By helping them navigate the complexities of the domain market, you can charge consulting fees and build a reputation as a trusted domain consultant.

Domain Auctions:

Participating in and profiting from online domain auctions is an exciting way to buy and sell domain names. By carefully selecting valuable domains and strategically bidding, you can secure profitable deals and maximize your earnings.

In conclusion, the world of domain flipping and digital product creation offers countless opportunities for entrepreneurs, students, fresh graduates, young entrepreneurs, and even parents looking to make some extra income. Whether you choose to buy and sell domain names, create websites, offer registration services, or provide expert advice, the potential for success and profitability in this niche is vast. So why not dive into the world of domain names and start flipping your fortune today?

Chapter 4: Domain Parking: Earning Money with Unused Domain Names

Understanding Domain Parking

Domain parking is a lesser-known but highly lucrative aspect of the domain flipping industry. In this subchapter, we will explore the concept of domain parking and how it can be used to earn money by displaying ads on unused domain names.

Domain parking essentially involves registering a domain name and then monetizing it by displaying relevant advertisements on the parked page. This is particularly useful for domain names that are not currently being used for any website or online business. Instead of leaving these domains idle, domain owners can park them and earn passive income through ad revenue.

For entrepreneurs, students, fresh graduates, young entrepreneurs, and even parents looking for additional sources of income, domain parking offers a relatively simple and hassle-free way to generate revenue. It requires minimal effort and can be done alongside other ventures or commitments.

To get started with domain parking, one needs to choose a reliable domain parking service provider. These platforms specialize in displaying targeted advertisements on parked domains and ensuring maximum revenue generation. Some popular domain parking companies include Sedo, Bodis, and ParkingCrew.

Once you have selected a domain parking service, you can sign up and start parking your unused domain names. The service provider will handle the process of displaying relevant ads on your parked pages and tracking the revenue generated. Depending on the popularity and traffic of your parked domains, you can earn a significant passive income.

Domain parking is an excellent option for individuals interested in the domain flipping niche and looking for a low-risk strategy to earn money from their domain investments. It allows you to monetize your parked domains while waiting for potential buyers or other opportunities to arise. Additionally, it can be a valuable learning experience for understanding the dynamics of online advertising and generating revenue through targeted ads.

In conclusion, domain parking is a profitable avenue within the domain flipping industry. It offers entrepreneurs, students, fresh graduates, young entrepreneurs, and parents a hassle-free way to earn passive income by displaying ads on unused domain names. By utilizing domain parking services and selecting high-quality advertisements, individuals can generate a steady stream of revenue while waiting for potential buyers or other opportunities to maximize their domain investments.

Choosing a Domain Parking Service

In the world of domain flipping, one of the key strategies for generating income is domain parking. This involves earning money by displaying ads on unused domain names. However, in order to effectively monetize your parked domains, it is crucial to choose the right domain parking service. Here are some important factors to consider when making this decision.

Firstly, you need to ensure that the domain parking service you choose offers a user-friendly platform. As an entrepreneur, student, fresh graduate, or young entrepreneur, you may not have extensive technical knowledge, so it is important to find a service that makes it easy for you to set up and manage your parked domains. Look for a service that offers a simple and intuitive interface, allowing you to quickly and easily add your domains and customize the ad settings.

Another important consideration is the revenue potential of the domain parking service. Different services offer varying levels of payouts, so it is crucial to compare the potential earnings before making a decision. Look for a service that offers competitive rates and has a track record of consistent payments. It is also worth considering whether the service offers additional monetization options, such as affiliate programs or direct ad sales, as this can further boost your earnings.

Additionally, it is important to choose a domain parking service that provides reliable support. As a parent or student, you may have limited time to devote to managing your parked domains, so it is essential to have a responsive support team that can assist you with any issues or questions that may arise. Look for a service that offers multiple channels of support, such as email, live chat, and phone, and check whether they have a reputation for providing timely and helpful assistance.

Lastly, consider the reputation and credibility of the domain parking service. As someone involved in the niche of making money from domain names, you need to ensure that the service you choose is reputable and trustworthy. Take the time to research the company, read reviews from other users, and check whether they have been involved in any controversies or scams in the past.

Choosing the right domain parking service is a crucial step in maximizing your earnings from domain flipping. By considering factors such as user-friendliness, revenue potential, support, and reputation, you can make an informed decision that will help you achieve success in the lucrative world of domain flipping.

Optimizing Ads for Maximum Revenue

In the ever-evolving world of digital advertising, optimizing ads for maximum revenue has become a crucial skill for anyone looking to make money in the domain flipping industry. Whether you are an entrepreneur, student, fresh graduate, young entrepreneur, or even a parent, understanding how to monetize your domain names through effective ad placement can significantly increase your profits.

One of the most popular ways to earn money from domain names is through domain parking. By displaying ads on unused domain names, you can generate a constant stream of revenue. However, simply parking your domains and hoping for the best won't cut it. To maximize your earnings, it's essential to optimize your ads.

First and foremost, you need to choose the right ad network. There are several options available, such as Google AdSense, Media.net, and Adsterra, each with its own strengths and weaknesses. Research and compare these networks to find the one that best suits your niche and target audience.

Next, you need to strategically place your ads. Experiment with different ad formats, sizes, and locations on your website to determine which combination generates the highest click-through rates and conversions. Remember, the key is to strike a balance between ad visibility and user experience. Too many ads can be overwhelming and drive visitors away, while too few may not generate enough revenue.

Additionally, consider targeting your ads to specific demographics or interests. Most ad networks provide targeting options that allow you to reach a more relevant audience. By displaying ads that align with your visitors' interests, you increase the chances of them clicking on the ads, resulting in higher revenue.

Regularly monitor your ad performance and make adjustments as needed. Analyze data such as click-through rates, conversion rates, and revenue generated to identify areas for improvement. Split testing different ad variations can also help you determine which ads are most effective in generating revenue.

Lastly, keep up with industry trends and stay informed about changes in ad policies and algorithms. This way, you can adapt your strategies accordingly and ensure that your ads remain optimized for maximum revenue.

In conclusion, optimizing ads for maximum revenue is a vital skill for anyone involved in domain flipping. By choosing the right ad network, strategically placing ads, targeting specific demographics, monitoring ad performance, and staying updated with industry trends, you can maximize your earnings and unlock the full potential of your domain names.

Tracking and Analyzing Domain Parking Performance

In the world of domain flipping, one of the strategies to generate income is through domain parking. Domain parking involves displaying ads on unused domain names to earn money. However, to maximize your earnings, it is crucial to track and analyze the performance of your parked domains. This subchapter will provide valuable insights into how you can effectively track and analyze the performance of your parked domains.

Tracking the performance of your parked domains is essential to identify which domains are generating revenue and which ones are underperforming. By monitoring the traffic, click-through rates, and conversion rates of your parked domains, you can make informed decisions about optimizing and monetizing them for maximum profitability.

There are various tools and platforms available that can help you track and analyze the performance of your parked domains. Google Analytics, for instance, allows you to track the traffic, demographics, and behavior of visitors to your parked domains. By analyzing this data, you can identify patterns, trends, and opportunities for improvement.

Furthermore, it is essential to analyze the performance of the ads displayed on your parked domains. By monitoring the click-through rates, conversion rates, and earnings per click, you can determine which ads are performing well and generating revenue. This information can help you optimize your ad placements and choose the most profitable ad networks for your parked domains.

In addition to tracking and analyzing the performance of your parked domains, it is also crucial to compare the performance of different domains in your portfolio. By identifying the high-performing domains, you can focus your efforts on optimizing and monetizing them further. On the other hand, if certain domains consistently underperform, you may consider selling or developing them into profitable websites or online businesses.

Tracking and analyzing the performance of your parked domains is a continuous process. It requires regular monitoring, data analysis, and optimization to ensure maximum profitability. By leveraging the right tracking tools and platforms, you can make data-driven decisions and optimize your domain parking strategy for success.

Whether you are an entrepreneur, student, fresh graduate, young entrepreneur, or parent, tracking and analyzing domain parking performance can be a valuable skill to generate income from domain names. By understanding the metrics and tools involved, you can make informed decisions about optimizing and monetizing your parked domains for maximum profitability.

Chapter 5: Domain Brokerage: Connecting Buyers and Sellers for Profit

Becoming a Domain Broker

In the ever-evolving world of online business, domain flipping has emerged as a lucrative opportunity for entrepreneurs, students, fresh graduates, young entrepreneurs, and even parents. One of the key roles in the domain flipping industry is that of a domain broker. This subchapter will shed light on the art of becoming a domain broker and how it can be a stepping stone towards financial success.

As a domain broker, your main task is to act as a middleman, connecting domain buyers and sellers for a commission. This role requires a keen eye for identifying valuable domain names and a strong understanding of market trends. By effectively matching buyers and sellers, you can earn substantial profits.

To become a successful domain broker, it is essential to develop a deep knowledge of the domain flipping industry. Stay updated with the latest trends, follow industry blogs, and join relevant forums to gain insights from experienced professionals. This knowledge will enable you to identify potential buyers and sellers, and negotiate profitable deals.

Building a strong network is crucial for any domain broker. Attend industry events, join online communities, and connect with individuals who are active in the domain flipping field. By establishing relationships with buyers and sellers, you can increase your chances of closing profitable deals and expanding your network further.

To enhance your credibility as a domain broker, consider obtaining certifications or accreditations in the field. This will not only boost your reputation but also provide you with valuable industry insights and resources. Additionally, offering additional services such as domain appraisal or consulting can differentiate you from competitors and attract more clients.

As a domain broker, it is important to stay ethical and transparent in your dealings. Maintain open communication with both buyers and sellers, ensuring that all parties are satisfied with the transaction. A positive reputation will not only attract more clients but also lead to repeat business and referrals.

In conclusion, becoming a domain broker offers a unique opportunity to profit from the domain flipping industry. By honing your skills, building a strong network, and offering exceptional service, you can establish yourself as a trusted middleman in the domain market. Embrace the art of domain brokering, and unlock the potential for financial success in this exciting field.

Building a Network of Buyers and Sellers

In today's digital age, the potential for making money online is vast, and one lucrative avenue worth exploring is domain flipping. Domain flipping involves buying and selling domain names for profit, and it can be a highly profitable venture if approached with the right strategy and knowledge.

To succeed in the domain flipping business, you need to build a network of buyers and sellers who are interested in the domain names you have to offer. This network will not only help you find potential buyers for your domains but also provide you with a steady supply of valuable domains to acquire and sell.

One way to start building your network is by participating in domain auctions. Online domain auctions are a great platform to connect with other domain investors and professionals in the industry. By actively participating in these auctions, you can showcase your expertise and establish relationships with potential buyers and sellers.

Another effective method to expand your network is by offering domain appraisal services. Many individuals and businesses are unsure about the value of their domain names and seek professional advice to make informed decisions. By providing domain appraisal services, you can position yourself as an expert in the field and attract potential buyers and sellers who value your expertise.

Additionally, consider offering domain consulting services to individuals or businesses looking for guidance on domain name strategies. As a consultant, you can leverage your knowledge and experience to help others make informed decisions about their domain investments. This not only builds your network but also establishes you as a trusted authority in the domain flipping industry.

Furthermore, actively networking with other entrepreneurs, students, fresh graduates, young entrepreneurs, and parents can also prove beneficial in building your network. Attend industry conferences, join online forums and communities, and engage in social media conversations related to domain flipping. By sharing your insights, experiences, and successes, you can attract like-minded individuals who may be interested in buying or selling domain names.

Remember that building a network takes time and effort. It requires consistent engagement, staying updated with industry trends, and offering value to your network. By actively participating in domain auctions, offering appraisal and consulting services, and networking with others in the domain flipping industry, you can create a strong network of buyers and sellers that will fuel your success as a domain flipper.

Whether you are an entrepreneur, student, fresh graduate, young entrepreneur, or parent, exploring the world of domain flipping can provide you with an exciting opportunity to make money online. By building a network of buyers and sellers, you can unlock the full potential of this business and pave your way to financial success.

Negotiating Deals and Closing Sales

In the world of domain flipping, the ability to negotiate deals and close sales is crucial to your success. Whether you are a seasoned entrepreneur, a student, a fresh graduate, a young entrepreneur, or a parent looking to make some extra income, mastering the art of negotiation will significantly impact your ability to profit from domain flipping.

One of the key strategies in negotiating deals is to do your research. Before entering any negotiation, it is essential to gather as much information as possible about the domain name you are interested in, its market value, and the potential buyers or sellers involved. This knowledge will give you leverage and confidence during the negotiation process.

When it comes to closing sales, it is vital to understand the psychology of your potential buyers. People are more likely to make a purchase when they feel a sense of urgency or scarcity. By highlighting the unique features or benefits of the domain name you are selling and creating a sense of exclusivity, you can increase the perceived value and motivate buyers to take action.

Another effective strategy in closing sales is to create win-win situations. Negotiations should not be seen as a zero-sum game, where one party wins at the expense of the other. Instead, focus on finding mutually beneficial agreements that satisfy the needs and desires of both parties. This approach builds trust and increases the likelihood of successful deal closure.

To enhance your negotiation and sales skills, consider exploring different niches within domain flipping. Whether you choose to make money from domain names, engage in domain brokerage, or invest in valuable domain names, each niche requires its own set of negotiation and sales techniques. By diversifying your knowledge and expertise, you can adapt to various situations and maximize your profit potential.

As you navigate the world of domain flipping, remember that negotiation and sales are not one-time events but ongoing processes. Constantly refining your skills, staying up-to-date with industry trends, and networking with other professionals will help you stay competitive and seize new opportunities.

In conclusion, negotiating deals and closing sales are essential skills for anyone involved in domain flipping. Whether you are a seasoned entrepreneur or a young graduate looking to make some extra income, mastering the art of negotiation will significantly impact your success in this industry. By researching, understanding the psychology of buyers, creating win-win situations, and exploring different niches within domain flipping, you can increase your profit potential and achieve your goals.

Ensuring a Smooth Transaction Process

When it comes to the art of domain flipping, one of the most crucial aspects is ensuring a smooth transaction process. Whether you are a seasoned entrepreneur, a student looking to make some extra money, a fresh graduate eager to enter the business world, a young entrepreneur with a passion for digital assets, or even a parent looking for a lucrative side hustle, understanding how to navigate the transaction process is essential.

In the world of domain flipping, there are various strategies you can employ to maximize your profits. From domain parking and brokerage to investing and development, the opportunities are endless. However, irrespective of the niche you choose, a smooth transaction process is vital to your success.

First and foremost, it is crucial to establish clear communication channels with potential buyers or sellers. Promptly responding to inquiries, negotiating prices, and addressing any concerns or questions are all part of ensuring a smooth transaction. Remember, in the fast-paced world of domain flipping, time is of the essence, and delays can cost you valuable opportunities.

Additionally, it is essential to have a secure and reliable payment system in place. With the rise of online scams and fraudulent activities, it is imperative to protect yourself and your assets. Utilize reputable payment platforms that offer buyer and seller protection to ensure a secure transaction.

Furthermore, conducting due diligence is key to avoiding any legal or ethical issues during the transaction process. Research the history of the domain, check for any trademark infringements, and ensure that all necessary documentation is in order. This will not only protect you legally but also build trust with potential buyers or sellers.

Finally, maintaining a professional and organized approach is essential. Keep detailed records of all transactions, including purchase agreements, transfer of ownership, and payment receipts. This will not only streamline the process but also provide you with a comprehensive record of your domain flipping activities.

In conclusion, ensuring a smooth transaction process is vital to the success of domain flipping. By establishing clear communication channels, utilizing secure payment systems, conducting due diligence, and maintaining a professional approach, you can navigate the intricacies of buying and selling domain names with ease. Whether you choose to specialize in domain parking, brokerage, investing, development, or any other niche, mastering the art of smooth transactions will undoubtedly contribute to your success in the competitive world of domain flipping.

Chapter 6: Domain Investing: Building a Valuable Portfolio

Strategies for Domain Investing

Domain investing has become a lucrative business opportunity for entrepreneurs, students, fresh graduates, young entrepreneurs, and even parents looking to make some extra income. This subchapter will explore various strategies to help you succeed in the world of domain investing.

1. Research and Analysis: Before investing in any domain, it is crucial to conduct thorough research and analysis. Look for popular keywords, trends, and emerging industries to identify potentially valuable domain names. Use tools like Google Trends, keyword planners, and domain appraisal services to assess the market value of a domain.

2. Diversify Your Portfolio: Building a diverse portfolio of domain names is essential for long-term success. Invest in different niches, industries, and trends to minimize risk and maximize potential returns. This approach ensures that you have a range of options to monetize your domains.

3. Buy Low, Sell High: One of the fundamental principles of domain flipping is buying low and selling high. Look for undervalued domain names in expired domain auctions or online marketplaces. Negotiate and acquire domains at a reasonable price, and then list them for sale at a higher price to generate a profit.

4. Develop and Monetize: Instead of just flipping domains, consider developing websites or online businesses on your purchased domain names. Create valuable content, optimize for search engines, and monetize through ad placements, affiliate marketing, or selling products/services. This approach can generate a steady stream of passive income.

5. Domain Parking: If you own unused domain names, consider parking them to earn money through display ads. Services like Google AdSense allow you to monetize your parked domains by displaying relevant advertisements. While the returns might not be as high as actively developed websites, it is an effortless way to earn passive income.

6. Be a Domain Broker: Act as a middleman connecting domain buyers and sellers. Offer your expertise in negotiating deals and facilitate domain transfers for a commission. Develop a network of potential buyers and sellers, and leverage your knowledge of the market to find profitable opportunities.

7. Stay Updated: The domain industry is constantly evolving, with new trends and technologies emerging regularly. Stay updated with industry news, attend domain conferences, and engage with domain communities online. This will help you spot upcoming opportunities and adapt your strategies accordingly.

Remember, domain investing requires patience, persistence, and a keen eye for potential opportunities. By implementing these strategies and staying committed to your goals, you can turn domain investing into a profitable venture. Whether you choose to flip domains, develop websites, or provide domain-related services, this subchapter will equip you with the knowledge and tools needed to succeed in the domain investing industry.

Identifying Valuable Domain Names

In the fast-paced digital age, the world of domain flipping has emerged as a lucrative opportunity for entrepreneurs, students, fresh graduates, young entrepreneurs, and even parents looking to make some extra income. But how do you identify valuable domain names that can fetch a high price in the market? This subchapter will guide you through the process of identifying valuable domain names and help you maximize your profits in the art of domain flipping.

One of the key factors in identifying valuable domain names is keyword research. Understanding popular search terms and trends can give you a competitive edge in selecting domain names that are in high demand. Use tools like Google Keyword Planner or SEMrush to analyze search volume and competition for specific keywords. By identifying keywords with high search volume and low competition, you can target domain names that are likely to attract a large audience.

Another approach to identifying valuable domain names is keeping an eye on emerging trends and industries. Stay updated with the latest technological advancements, popular products, or emerging markets. By acquiring domain names related to these trends, you can capitalize on the growing demand and sell them at a premium price.

Additionally, it is crucial to consider the length and memorability of your domain names. Short, catchy, and easy-to-remember domain names are more likely to attract potential buyers. Avoid using hyphens or numbers in your domain names as they can create confusion and make it harder for users to remember.

Furthermore, conducting thorough market research and analyzing the potential profitability of a domain name is essential. Look for similar domain names that have been sold in the past and evaluate their selling price. This will give you an idea of the market value and demand for similar domain names.

Lastly, consider the branding potential of a domain name. A domain name that aligns with a specific niche or industry has the potential to become a brand in itself. Buyers are often willing to pay a premium price for domain names with branding potential.

By implementing these strategies and staying informed about the latest trends and market demands, you can become a skilled domain flipper. Remember, identifying valuable domain names is just the first step; the real art lies in negotiating skillfully and marketing your domain names effectively to maximize your profits. So, dive into the world of domain flipping and unlock the potential to flip your fortune!

Building and Managing a Domain Portfolio

In the ever-evolving world of the internet, domain flipping has emerged as a lucrative business opportunity for entrepreneurs, students, fresh graduates, young entrepreneurs, and even parents. This subchapter, titled "Building and Managing a Domain Portfolio," will guide you through the various aspects of this exciting field and help you navigate the path to success.

One of the first steps in building a domain portfolio is understanding the different niches within the domain flipping industry. Whether you are interested in making money from domain names, domain flipping, domain parking, domain brokerage, domain investing, domain development, domain monetization, domain registration services, domain appraisal, domain consulting, or domain auctions, this subchapter will provide valuable insights and strategies for each niche.

To start, it is essential to research and identify valuable domain names that have the potential for high returns. This can involve analyzing trends, keyword research, and understanding the target audience. Once you have acquired these domain names, it is crucial to manage them effectively. This includes keeping track of expiration dates, renewing domains, and optimizing their potential for profitability.

Domain development is another avenue to explore. By creating websites or online businesses on purchased domain names, you can generate revenue through advertising, e-commerce, or other monetization methods. This subchapter will provide practical tips on website development, content creation, and search engine optimization to maximize your domain's potential.

Furthermore, domain monetization strategies, such as optimizing existing websites or blogs with valuable domain names, can significantly increase your income. This subchapter will delve into various monetization methods, including ad placement, affiliate marketing, sponsored content, and more.

Additionally, this subchapter will discuss domain registration services and the potential income you can earn through registration fees. It will also shed light on domain appraisal services, which can help you determine the value of domain names for buyers and sellers. By offering domain appraisal services, you can position yourself as an expert in the industry and attract potential clients.

Lastly, this subchapter will explore the world of domain auctions. Participating in online domain auctions can be a thrilling way to profit from buying and selling domain names. It will provide you with strategies to identify undervalued domains, negotiate deals, and ultimately flip them for a profit.

Whether you are new to domain flipping or looking to expand your existing portfolio, this subchapter will equip you with the knowledge and tools necessary to succeed in the art of domain flipping. By following the strategies outlined and taking advantage of the various niches within the industry, you can turn your domain portfolio into a lucrative source of income.

Capitalizing on Domain Appreciation and Sales

In the fast-paced world of the internet, domain names have become valuable assets that can be bought and sold for a significant profit. If you're looking for a lucrative opportunity to make money online, the art of domain flipping is a skill worth mastering. Whether you're an entrepreneur, student, fresh graduate, young entrepreneur, or even a parent seeking a new source of income, this subchapter on capitalizing on domain appreciation and sales will guide you through the exciting world of domain flipping.

Domain flipping involves buying domain names at a low price and selling them at a higher price, taking advantage of their appreciation over time. This niche offers various avenues for making money, such as domain parking, brokerage, investing, development, monetization, registration services, appraisal, consulting, and participating in domain auctions. Let's explore some of these strategies in more detail.

If you have unused domain names, domain parking allows you to earn money by displaying ads on them. By optimizing and monetizing your existing websites or blogs with valuable domain names, you can generate revenue through advertising and other monetization techniques. Alternatively, you can act as a middleman in domain brokerage, connecting buyers and sellers and earning a commission for facilitating successful transactions.

If you have a knack for identifying valuable domain names, domain investing might be your calling. Build a portfolio of valuable domain names and earn income through their appreciation over time. Domain development is another option, where you create websites or online businesses on purchased domain names to generate revenue through e-commerce, advertising, or other online business models.

For those with expertise in the field, offering domain appraisal or consulting services can be highly profitable. Buyers and sellers often require professional advice to determine the value of their domain names or develop effective domain strategies. You can provide expert guidance and charge a fee for your services.

Lastly, participating in online domain auctions can be a thrilling way to profit from domain flipping. By acquiring valuable domain names at auction and reselling them, you can capitalize on the demand for desirable domain names.

Regardless of your background or experience, domain flipping offers a range of opportunities to make money from domain names. With the right knowledge, strategy, and perseverance, you can turn this art into a profitable venture. This subchapter will equip you with the essential skills and insights needed to succeed in the exciting world of domain flipping.

Chapter 7: Domain Development: Generating Revenue with Websites

Understanding Domain Development

In the ever-expanding digital world, the potential for making money is limitless. One avenue that has gained significant traction in recent years is domain development. This subchapter will delve into the intricacies of domain development and how it can be a lucrative venture for entrepreneurs, students, fresh graduates, young entrepreneurs, and even parents looking to generate additional income.

Domain development encompasses the creation of websites or online businesses on purchased domain names with the aim of generating revenue. This subchapter will explore various strategies and techniques that can be employed to maximize the potential of these digital assets.

One approach to domain development is to create niche-specific websites or blogs that cater to a particular audience. By providing valuable content, attracting visitors, and optimizing the website for search engines, entrepreneurs can monetize their domain names through advertising, sponsored posts, and affiliate marketing.

Another avenue for domain development is to leverage unused domain names by displaying ads on them. This practice, known as domain parking, allows individuals to earn passive income while they explore other opportunities. The subchapter will delve into the best practices for optimizing domain parking and maximizing revenue from these underutilized assets.

Furthermore, domain brokerage can be a lucrative endeavor for those with strong negotiation skills. Acting as a middleman, individuals can connect domain buyers and sellers and earn a commission based on the successful transaction. This subchapter will provide valuable insights into the domain brokerage process and offer tips on how to become a successful domain broker.

Additionally, domain investing, similar to real estate investing, involves building a portfolio of valuable domain names and earning income through their appreciation. The subchapter will highlight the key factors to consider when investing in domain names, such as market trends, keyword relevance, and brandability.

Lastly, the subchapter will explore other domain-related income streams, such as domain registration services, domain appraisal, domain consulting, and domain auctions. These avenues provide alternative ways to generate revenue from domain names, and the subchapter will offer valuable guidance on how to tap into these opportunities.

Whether you are an entrepreneur, student, fresh graduate, young entrepreneur, or a parent looking to make money online, understanding domain development is crucial. This subchapter will equip you with the knowledge and strategies needed to navigate the domain development landscape, maximize the potential of your domain names, and ultimately flip your fortune.

Choosing a Niche for Website Development

When it comes to website development, choosing the right niche is crucial for success. Whether you are an entrepreneur, student, fresh graduate, young entrepreneur, or even a parent looking to make some extra income, understanding the various niches in website development can help you make informed decisions and maximize your profits. In this subchapter, we will explore different niches within the domain flipping industry and discuss their potential for generating revenue.

One lucrative niche is "Make Money From Domain Names." This involves acquiring domain names with the intention of selling them for a profit. We will delve into strategies for finding valuable domain names and understanding market trends to ensure a successful flip.

Another niche is "Domain flipping: Buying and selling domain names for profit." This involves buying domain names at a lower price and selling them at a higher price. We will explore effective negotiation techniques and online platforms where you can buy and sell domain names.

"Domain parking: Earning money by displaying ads on unused domain names" is another niche worth considering. We will discuss how to optimize unused domain names by displaying ads and earning passive income from them.

For those interested in being a middleman, "Domain brokerage: Acting as a middleman to connect domain buyers and sellers for a commission" is an excellent niche. We will guide you on how to establish yourself as a reliable broker and earn a commission by connecting domain buyers and sellers.

If you prefer a long-term investment strategy, "Domain investing: Building a portfolio of valuable domain names and earning income through their appreciation" may be the niche for you. We will provide insights into identifying valuable domain names and strategies for building a successful portfolio.

Moreover, we will explore the niche of "Domain development: Creating websites or online businesses on purchased domain names to generate revenue." This involves building websites or online businesses on purchased domain names to generate revenue through advertising, affiliate marketing, or selling products/services.

Other niches we will discuss include "Domain monetization," "Domain registration services," "Domain appraisal," "Domain consulting," and "Domain auctions." These niches offer various opportunities for generating income and require different skill sets and strategies.

By understanding these niches and their potential, you can make informed decisions and choose the niche that aligns with your skills, interests, and goals. Whether you are looking for a side hustle or a full-time business, the world of domain flipping offers endless opportunities for success. Stay tuned for more in-depth discussions on each niche in the following chapters.

Building and Designing Profitable Websites

In the ever-evolving digital landscape, having a strong online presence is crucial for any business or individual looking to make money and succeed in the modern world. One of the most effective ways to establish this online presence is through building and designing profitable websites. In this subchapter, we will explore the various strategies and opportunities available in the realm of website development, specifically focusing on the art of domain flipping.

Domain flipping, also known as buying and selling domain names for profit, has emerged as a lucrative business venture for entrepreneurs, students, fresh graduates, and young entrepreneurs. This niche market offers a range of opportunities to make money, including domain parking, domain brokerage, domain investing, domain development, domain monetization, and more.

For those interested in making money from domain names, domain flipping is an excellent starting point. By purchasing unused domain names and displaying relevant ads, individuals can earn money through domain parking. Additionally, acting as a middleman to connect domain buyers and sellers for a commission is a viable option through domain brokerage.

Domain investing involves building a portfolio of valuable domain names and earning income through their appreciation. On the other hand, domain development focuses on creating websites or online businesses on purchased domain names to generate revenue. By optimizing and monetizing existing websites or blogs with valuable domain names, individuals can further explore domain monetization strategies.

Furthermore, entrepreneurs can consider offering domain registration services, earning income through registration fees. Additionally, providing domain appraisal services to determine the value of domain names for buyers and sellers is another avenue to explore through domain appraisal. Expert advice and guidance on domain name strategies can be offered through domain consulting services.

Lastly, participating in and profiting from online domain auctions by buying and selling domain names is yet another way to make money in the domain flipping industry.

In conclusion, building and designing profitable websites offers a range of opportunities to make money from domain names. Whether through domain flipping, domain parking, domain brokerage, domain investing, domain development, domain monetization, domain registration services, domain appraisal, domain consulting, or domain auctions, individuals can explore various strategies and niches to generate income and achieve success in the digital world.

Driving Traffic and Monetizing Websites

In today's digital age, the potential for making money online is vast. One lucrative avenue that many entrepreneurs, students, fresh graduates, young entrepreneurs, and even parents are exploring is the world of domain flipping. This subchapter explores various ways to drive traffic to your website and monetize it effectively.

One of the main ways to generate income from domain names is through domain flipping. This involves buying and selling domain names for profit. By purchasing undervalued domain names and reselling them at a higher price, you can turn a significant profit. This niche is perfect for those with a keen eye for identifying valuable domain names and understanding market trends.

Another method of making money from domain names is through domain parking. This involves earning money by displaying ads on unused domain names. By using a domain parking service, you can monetize your domains and earn passive income without having to invest time and effort into developing a website.

If you have a knack for sales and negotiation, consider becoming a domain broker. Acting as a middleman to connect domain buyers and sellers for a commission can be highly profitable. By leveraging your network and marketing skills, you can earn a substantial income by facilitating domain transactions.

Domain investing is another avenue to explore. By building a portfolio of valuable domain names and earning income through their appreciation, you can create a long-term revenue stream. This requires research, analysis, and an understanding of market trends, but the potential rewards can be substantial.

For those with a passion for website development, creating websites or online businesses on purchased domain names can generate revenue. By utilizing effective marketing strategies, search engine optimization, and monetization techniques, you can attract traffic and monetize your website through ads, affiliate marketing, or selling products and services.

If you have technical expertise, offering domain registration services can also be lucrative. By becoming a domain registrar and earning income through registration fees, you can tap into a steady revenue stream.

Other ways to monetize domain names include providing appraisal services to determine the value of domain names for buyers and sellers, offering expert advice and guidance as a domain consultant, and participating in online domain auctions.

In conclusion, the world of domain flipping offers numerous opportunities for entrepreneurs, students, fresh graduates, young entrepreneurs, and even parents to make money online. Whether through buying and selling domain names, domain parking, domain brokerage, domain investing, domain development, domain monetization, domain registration services, domain appraisal, domain consulting, or domain auctions, there are plenty of ways to drive traffic and monetize websites. With dedication, research, and a willingness to adapt to changing market trends, you can flip your fortune in the art of domain flipping.

Chapter 8: Domain Monetization: Maximizing Revenue from Existing Websites

Evaluating the Potential of Existing Websites

In the world of domain flipping, it is essential to have a keen eye for identifying the potential of existing websites. When it comes to evaluating the value and profitability of a website, there are several factors that entrepreneurs, students, fresh graduates, young entrepreneurs, and even parents should consider. By understanding the potential of existing websites, you can make informed decisions and maximize your profits in the domain flipping industry.

One crucial aspect to evaluate is the website's traffic and audience engagement. A website with a consistent flow of organic traffic indicates its popularity and relevance. Look for websites that attract a specific niche audience, as this often translates to higher demand and potential for monetization. Analyzing the website's traffic sources, such as search engines or social media platforms, can give you insights into its reach and potential for growth.

Another factor to consider is the website's revenue streams. Evaluate how the website currently generates income, whether it's through display ads, affiliate marketing, or selling products and services. Websites that have diversified revenue streams are often more valuable and have the potential for future growth. Assess the website's conversion rates and average revenue per user to gauge its profitability.

Furthermore, examine the website's design and user experience. A well-designed and user-friendly website attracts more visitors and encourages them to stay longer, resulting in higher engagement and potential revenue. Evaluate the website's navigation, layout, and overall aesthetics to determine if any improvements are required to enhance its potential.

While evaluating the potential of existing websites, it is crucial to research the niche and competition. Understand the market demand and trends within the website's niche to determine its long-term viability. Analyze the competition and identify opportunities for differentiation and improvement. This research will help you make informed decisions about whether to invest in a website and how to maximize its potential.

Lastly, consider the website's search engine optimization (SEO) potential. A website that ranks well in search engine results has a higher chance of attracting organic traffic and generating revenue. Evaluate the website's on-page SEO elements, such as keyword optimization and meta tags, as well as its backlink profile. Determine if there are any opportunities for SEO optimization to increase the website's visibility and potential profitability.

By thoroughly evaluating the potential of existing websites, entrepreneurs, students, fresh graduates, young entrepreneurs, and even parents can make smart investment decisions in the domain flipping industry. Understanding the website's traffic, revenue streams, design, niche, competition, and SEO potential will enable you to identify valuable opportunities and maximize your profits in this lucrative field.

Optimizing Websites for Increased Revenue

In today's digital age, having a strong online presence is crucial for the success of any business. With the ever-growing popularity and importance of domain names, entrepreneurs, students, fresh graduates, young entrepreneurs, and even parents can tap into the lucrative world of domain flipping to generate substantial revenue.

Domain flipping involves buying and selling domain names for profit. However, simply owning valuable domain names is not enough to maximize your earnings. To truly unlock the potential of your domain portfolio, optimizing websites is essential.

One of the most effective ways to optimize a website is through domain parking. By displaying targeted ads on unused domain names, you can earn money passively. This strategy is particularly useful if you have a large number of underutilized domains in your portfolio.

Another strategy to consider is domain development. By creating websites or online businesses on purchased domain names, you can generate revenue through various means such as advertising, affiliate marketing, or e-commerce. This approach allows you to capitalize on the value of your domain names by turning them into profitable ventures.

Additionally, domain monetization is an excellent way to optimize existing websites or blogs with valuable domain names. By implementing strategies like search engine optimization (SEO), content marketing, and affiliate partnerships, you can increase traffic and revenue on your website.

For those with a passion for advising and guiding others, domain consulting can be a lucrative niche. Offering expert advice on domain name strategies to individuals or businesses can be highly sought after, especially in a market where domain names are becoming increasingly valuable.

Furthermore, participating in domain auctions can be a profitable venture. By honing your skills in evaluating the value of domain names and understanding market trends, you can buy and sell domain names at auctions, capitalizing on the demand for specific domains.

Whether you choose to specialize in domain flipping, domain parking, domain development, or any other niche related to domain names, optimizing your websites is crucial for increased revenue. By implementing effective strategies and staying abreast of industry trends, you can maximize the potential of your domain portfolio and ultimately flip your fortune.

Implementing Effective Monetization Strategies

Monetizing domain names can be a lucrative venture for entrepreneurs, students, fresh graduates, young entrepreneurs, and even parents looking to generate extra income. In this subchapter, we will explore various effective monetization strategies that can be implemented to maximize profits in the domain flipping industry.

One of the most popular strategies is domain parking. This involves displaying ads on unused domain names, earning money every time someone clicks on those ads. By strategically selecting high-value domain names and optimizing them with relevant ads, individuals can generate a steady stream of income.

For those interested in connecting domain buyers and sellers, domain brokerage is a viable option. Acting as a middleman, entrepreneurs can earn a commission by successfully facilitating domain transactions. This requires a deep understanding of market trends, negotiation skills, and effective communication to ensure both parties benefit from the transaction.

Domain investing is another strategy that involves building a portfolio of valuable domain names and earning income through their appreciation. By conducting thorough research on emerging trends, industries, and popular keywords, individuals can acquire domain names that are in high demand. These domains can then be sold at a significant profit when the demand increases.

Domain development is yet another avenue for monetizing domain names. By creating websites or online businesses on purchased domain names, entrepreneurs can generate revenue through various means such as advertising, affiliate marketing, or selling products and services. This strategy requires a combination of web development skills, marketing expertise, and content creation to attract and retain a steady stream of visitors.

Domain monetization involves optimizing and monetizing existing websites or blogs with valuable domain names. By leveraging the traffic and authority of these websites, individuals can implement various monetization methods such as display advertising, sponsored content, or selling products and services.

Other strategies include offering domain registration services and earning income through registration fees, providing domain appraisal services to determine the value of domain names for buyers and sellers, offering expert advice and guidance on domain name strategies through domain consulting, and participating in and profiting from online domain auctions by buying and selling domain names.

In conclusion, implementing effective monetization strategies is crucial for success in the domain flipping industry. By carefully selecting the most suitable strategy based on individual skills, interests, and market trends, entrepreneurs, students, fresh graduates, young entrepreneurs, and even parents can generate a substantial income from domain names.

Tracking and Analyzing Website Performance

In the fast-paced world of online business, tracking and analyzing website performance is a crucial aspect of achieving success. As an entrepreneur, student, fresh graduate, young entrepreneur, or even a parent looking to make some extra money, understanding the ins and outs of website performance can greatly impact your ability to generate revenue from domain names.

Whether you are involved in domain flipping, domain parking, domain brokerage, domain investing, domain development, domain monetization, domain registration services, domain appraisal, domain consulting, or domain auctions, tracking and analyzing website performance is essential for making informed decisions and optimizing your efforts.

One of the key aspects of tracking website performance is monitoring website traffic. By utilizing tools such as Google Analytics, you can gain valuable insights into the number of visitors your website receives, where they are coming from, and how they are interacting with your site. This information allows you to identify trends, target specific demographics, and adjust your marketing strategies accordingly.

Additionally, tracking website performance involves analyzing conversion rates. Whether your goal is to sell domain names, display ads, or generate revenue through online businesses, understanding how many visitors are taking desired actions is crucial. By tracking conversion rates, you can identify areas for improvement and implement strategies to increase conversions.

Furthermore, tracking and analyzing website performance involves monitoring website speed and performance. Slow-loading websites can lead to high bounce rates and dissatisfied visitors. By regularly monitoring website speed and performance, you can ensure that your website is optimized for a seamless user experience.

In conclusion, tracking and analyzing website performance is a vital aspect of success in the domain industry. Whether you are involved in domain flipping, domain parking, domain brokerage, domain investing, domain development, domain monetization, domain registration services, domain appraisal, domain consulting, or domain auctions, understanding how to track and analyze website performance can greatly enhance your ability to generate revenue. By monitoring website traffic, analyzing conversion rates, and optimizing website speed and performance, you can make informed decisions and maximize your profits.

Chapter 9: Domain Registration Services: Starting Your Own Domain Registration Business

Researching the Domain Registration Industry

In the fast-paced world of technology and online business, the domain registration industry plays a crucial role. Whether you are an entrepreneur, student, fresh graduate, young entrepreneur, or even a parent looking for extra income, understanding the domain registration industry can open up a world of opportunities for you. In this subchapter, we will explore the various aspects of this industry and how you can leverage it to your advantage.

Make Money From Domain Names: One of the most lucrative niches within the domain registration industry is domain flipping. This involves buying and selling domain names for profit. By conducting thorough research and identifying valuable domain names, you can make a significant return on your investment.

Domain Parking: If you own unused domain names, you can earn money by displaying ads on them. This is known as domain parking. By optimizing your parked domains and attracting traffic, you can generate a passive income stream.

Domain Brokerage: Acting as a middleman between domain buyers and sellers can be a profitable venture. By connecting the right parties and earning a commission, you can capitalize on the growing demand for valuable domain names.

Domain Investing: Building a portfolio of valuable domain names is another strategy for earning income. As the value of domain names appreciates over time, you can sell them at a higher price or earn income through leasing or licensing agreements.

Domain Development: If you have the skills and resources, creating websites or online businesses on purchased domain names can generate substantial revenue. By monetizing these platforms through advertising, e-commerce, or other revenue streams, you can maximize your returns.

Domain Monetization: If you already own websites or blogs with valuable domain names, optimizing and monetizing them can be a great source of income. By implementing effective SEO strategies, attracting a larger audience, and leveraging advertising networks, you can generate passive income from your existing online properties.

Domain Registration Services: Offering domain registration services can be a lucrative business opportunity. By providing individuals and businesses with the ability to register their desired domain names, you can earn income through registration fees.

Domain Appraisal: As the demand for valuable domain names grows, providing domain appraisal services can be a profitable niche. By leveraging your expertise, you can help buyers and sellers determine the value of domain names and facilitate fair transactions.

Domain Consulting: Offering expert advice and guidance on domain name strategies can be a valuable service. As businesses and individuals seek to establish their online presence, your expertise can help them make informed decisions and maximize their investments.

Domain Auctions: Participating in online domain auctions presents an opportunity to profit from buying and selling domain names. By staying updated on industry trends and conducting thorough research, you can identify undervalued domains and capitalize on their potential.

Researching the domain registration industry is essential for anyone looking to enter the world of domain flipping, investing, or offering related services. By understanding the niches within this industry and identifying the most profitable opportunities, you can leverage your skills and resources to maximize your income potential.

Setting up a Domain Registration Service

If you're looking to start a profitable business in the domain industry, setting up a domain registration service can be a lucrative option. With more and more individuals and businesses realizing the importance of having an online presence, the demand for domain names is constantly growing. This subchapter will guide you through the process of establishing your own domain registration service, providing you with the necessary tools and knowledge to succeed in this industry.

To begin, it's crucial to understand the basics of domain registration. As a domain registration service, you will act as a registrar, allowing your customers to secure and manage their desired domain names. This involves partnering with an accredited domain registrar, which will handle the technical aspects of registration while you focus on customer service and marketing.

One of the first steps in setting up your domain registration service is choosing a reliable registrar partner. Look for a registrar with a solid reputation, competitive pricing, and robust management tools. This partnership will allow you to offer a wide range of domain extensions and ensure seamless registration processes.

Once you have established your registrar partnership, it's time to build your online presence. Create a user-friendly website that showcases your domain registration services, highlighting the benefits of choosing your service over competitors. Incorporate an intuitive domain search function, allowing users to quickly check the availability of their desired domain names.

Marketing your domain registration service is essential to attract customers. Utilize various online marketing strategies, such as search engine optimization, social media advertising, and content marketing, to reach your target audience. Identify your niche within the domain industry, whether it's catering to entrepreneurs, students, or fresh graduates, and tailor your marketing efforts accordingly.

Offering competitive pricing and excellent customer support will set you apart from the competition. Ensure that your pricing structure is transparent and reasonable, providing different packages to cater to different customers' needs. A responsive customer support system, through email, live chat, or phone, will instill trust in your customers and encourage them to choose your service.

Additionally, consider diversifying your revenue streams by offering complementary services such as domain parking, domain appraisal, or domain consulting. This will not only increase your income potential but also attract a wider range of customers.

In conclusion, setting up a domain registration service can be a profitable venture in the domain industry. By partnering with an accredited registrar, building a user-friendly website, implementing effective marketing strategies, and providing excellent customer support, you can establish a successful business in this niche. Stay up to date with industry trends and continuously adapt your services to meet the evolving needs of your customers.

Marketing and Attracting Customers

In the world of domain flipping, where success lies in buying and selling domain names for profit, attracting customers is essential. Whether you are an entrepreneur, student, fresh graduate, young entrepreneur, or even a parent looking to make some extra income, understanding the art of marketing is crucial to your success. This subchapter explores various strategies to help you effectively market your domain names and attract potential buyers.

One approach to consider is domain parking, where you earn money by displaying ads on unused domain names. By optimizing these parked domains with relevant ads and content, you can attract targeted traffic and increase the likelihood of generating revenue. Additionally, you can explore domain brokerage, acting as a middleman to connect domain buyers and sellers for a commission. Building a strong network and promoting your brokerage services will help you attract clients and facilitate successful transactions.

Another avenue to explore is domain investing, where you build a portfolio of valuable domain names and earn income through their appreciation. Marketing your portfolio to potential buyers, showcasing their value and potential, will increase the likelihood of attracting interested parties. Similarly, domain development involves creating websites or online businesses on purchased domain names to generate revenue. By marketing these developed domains effectively, you can attract customers who see the potential in your website or online business.

Domain monetization is another strategy to consider. By optimizing and monetizing existing websites or blogs with valuable domain names, you can generate passive income. Marketing your monetized websites or blogs through various channels, such as search engine optimization and social media, will help attract visitors and increase your chances of earning from your domain investments.

Additionally, you may consider offering domain registration services. By marketing your registration services and showcasing the benefits of registering domains through your platform, you can attract customers seeking reliable and efficient domain registration. Similarly, offering domain appraisal services will attract buyers and sellers seeking expert advice on determining the value of domain names.

For those with in-depth knowledge and experience in the domain industry, domain consulting is a niche worth exploring. By offering expert advice and guidance on domain name strategies, you can attract individuals and businesses seeking to maximize their investments in domain names.

Lastly, participating in domain auctions can be a lucrative way to profit from buying and selling domain names. By effectively marketing your domain auction listings and establishing a reputation as a reliable and knowledgeable auction participant, you can attract potential buyers and increase your chances of making profitable sales.

In conclusion, marketing and attracting customers is crucial in the world of domain flipping. By utilizing various strategies such as domain parking, brokerage, investing, development, monetization, registration, appraisal, consulting, and auctions, you can effectively promote your domain names and attract potential buyers. With the right marketing approach, you can maximize your profits and establish yourself as a successful domain flipper.

Managing and Growing Your Domain Registration Business

In the fast-paced world of online businesses, domain registration has emerged as a lucrative industry. With the right strategies and knowledge, you can turn your domain registration business into a successful venture. Whether you are an entrepreneur, student, fresh graduate, young entrepreneur, or even a parent looking to explore new opportunities, this subchapter will provide you with valuable insights on managing and growing your domain registration business.

One of the key aspects of a domain registration business is understanding the different niches within the domain industry. By familiarizing yourself with various domains, such as Make Money From Domain Names, Domain flipping, Domain parking, Domain brokerage, Domain investing, Domain development, Domain monetization, Domain registration services, Domain appraisal, Domain consulting, and Domain auctions, you can identify the areas that align with your expertise and interests.

To effectively manage your domain registration business, it is essential to stay updated with industry trends and market demands. Continuous learning and staying informed about new domain extensions, market trends, and emerging technologies will give you a competitive edge. This knowledge can help you make informed decisions when it comes to acquiring and registering domain names.

Building a strong network is crucial for the growth of your domain registration business. Engage with other professionals, attend industry conferences, and join online communities to connect with potential buyers and sellers. Collaborating with domain brokers, developers, and investors can open up new opportunities and expand your reach.

Customer satisfaction should be a top priority for your domain registration business. Provide excellent customer service, timely support, and transparent pricing to build trust and loyalty among your clients. By offering additional services like domain appraisal, consulting, and development, you can cater to a wider range of customer needs and increase revenue streams.

Marketing plays a vital role in the growth of any business. Utilize various marketing channels, such as social media, content marketing, and search engine optimization (SEO), to promote your domain registration services. Create engaging content that educates your target audience about the value of domains and the benefits of working with a reputable registration service.

As your domain registration business expands, consider automating processes and investing in reliable infrastructure to streamline operations. This will enable you to handle a larger volume of registrations and provide a seamless experience to your customers.

In conclusion, managing and growing a domain registration business requires a combination of industry knowledge, networking, customer-centric approach, marketing strategies, and efficient operations. By implementing these strategies, you can take your domain registration business to new heights and capitalize on the opportunities presented by the dynamic domain industry.

Chapter 10: Domain Appraisal: Determining the Value of Domain Names

Understanding Domain Appraisal

In the world of domain flipping, understanding the value of domain names is crucial to your success. Domain appraisal plays a vital role in determining the worth of a domain name and can greatly impact your buying and selling decisions. In this subchapter, we will delve into the intricacies of domain appraisal and provide you with the knowledge you need to make informed choices.

Domain appraisal is the process of evaluating the value of a domain name. It takes into consideration various factors such as the domain's length, keyword relevance, brandability, search engine optimization potential, and market trends. By understanding these factors, you can accurately assess the worth of a domain name and determine its potential for profitability.

For entrepreneurs, students, fresh graduates, young entrepreneurs, and even parents, domain appraisal can open up a world of opportunities. It can help you identify undervalued domain names that have the potential to be sold at a higher price, or it can assist you in deciding whether a domain name you own is worth selling or developing.

Domain appraisal is particularly relevant to those interested in the niches of making money from domain names, domain flipping, domain investing, and domain brokerage. By understanding the value of a domain name, you can negotiate better deals, attract potential buyers or sellers, and maximize your profits.

Additionally, domain appraisal can also be beneficial for individuals interested in domain development, domain monetization, and domain registration services. It helps you determine the potential revenue-generating capabilities of a domain name, whether through developing a website or blog, displaying ads on unused domains, or offering registration services.

For those looking for expert advice and guidance, domain consulting is another niche that can benefit from domain appraisal knowledge. By understanding the appraisal process, you can offer valuable insights to individuals or businesses on domain name strategies, helping them make informed decisions that align with their goals.

Lastly, domain auctions are a popular platform for buying and selling domain names. Understanding domain appraisal can give you an edge in these auctions. You can accurately assess the value of a domain name, bid strategically, and profit from the buying and selling process.

In conclusion, domain appraisal is a crucial aspect of domain flipping. It allows you to accurately assess the value of domain names, make informed buying and selling decisions, and maximize your profits. Whether you are an entrepreneur, student, fresh graduate, young entrepreneur, or even a parent, understanding domain appraisal can open up a world of opportunities in various niches such as domain flipping, domain investing, domain brokerage, and more.

Evaluating Factors that Influence Domain Value

In the world of domain flipping, understanding the factors that influence domain value is crucial to your success as an entrepreneur, student, fresh graduate, young entrepreneur, or even as a parent looking to make some extra income. Whether you are interested in domain flipping, domain parking, domain brokerage, domain investing, domain development, domain monetization, domain registration services, domain appraisal, domain consulting, or domain auctions, knowing how to evaluate the value of a domain name is essential.

One of the first factors to consider is the domain name itself. Is it catchy? Is it memorable? Does it reflect a popular keyword or industry? A domain name that is short, easy to pronounce, and directly related to a popular topic or business niche will generally have a higher value. Additionally, domain names that include commonly searched keywords or phrases will attract more organic traffic and therefore have a higher potential for generating revenue.

Another important factor to consider is the domain extension. While .com is still the most popular and widely recognized extension, other extensions such as .net, .org, and country-specific extensions can also hold value depending on the target audience and industry. However, it is important to note that certain domain extensions may have restrictions on who can register them, which can affect their marketability.

Domain age also plays a significant role in determining value. Older domains are generally considered more valuable as they have a longer history and are often associated with more credibility and trustworthiness. However, it is important to note that the age of a domain alone is not enough to determine its value. Factors such as the domain's history, previous content, and any past penalties or blacklisting should also be taken into account.

Furthermore, the demand for specific domain names within a particular industry or niche can greatly influence their value. Researching current trends and popular keywords in your chosen niche can help you identify domain names that are likely to have a high demand and, therefore, command a higher price.

Lastly, the overall market conditions and economic factors should be considered. The value of domain names, like any other asset, can fluctuate depending on market trends, economic conditions, and demand. Staying up-to-date with industry news, attending domain auctions, and networking with other domain investors can help you stay informed about current market trends and make more informed decisions.

In conclusion, evaluating the factors that influence domain value is essential for anyone interested in making money from domain names. By considering the domain name itself, the extension, age, demand, and market conditions, you can make more informed decisions when buying, selling, or investing in domain names. Remember, knowledge is power, and understanding these factors will give you a competitive edge in the world of domain flipping.

Utilizing Tools and Resources for Domain Appraisal

In the world of domain flipping, knowing the true value of a domain name is essential for making profitable decisions. Whether you are an entrepreneur, student, fresh graduate, young entrepreneur, or even a parent looking to make some extra income, understanding how to appraise domain names can be a valuable skill. Fortunately, there are various tools and resources available to help you in this process.

One of the most commonly used tools for domain appraisal is a domain valuation tool. These tools analyze various factors such as domain age, keyword relevance, search engine optimization potential, and market demand to estimate the value of a domain name. Some popular domain valuation tools include Estibot, GoDaddy Domain Appraisal, and Sedo.

In addition to these tools, it is important to stay up-to-date with market trends and industry news. Websites and forums dedicated to the domain flipping niche can provide valuable insights into recent sales, emerging trends, and potential buyers. By immersing yourself in these communities, you can gain a deeper understanding of the market and make more informed appraisal decisions.

Another valuable resource for domain appraisal is professional domain brokers. These experts have extensive experience in the domain industry and can provide expert advice on pricing, negotiation strategies, and potential buyers. Working with a domain broker can help you maximize the value of your domain names and increase your chances of making a profitable sale.

Furthermore, attending domain auctions can be an excellent way to gauge the value of domain names. By participating in these auctions, you can observe the bidding patterns and final sale prices of similar domains. This firsthand experience can give you a better understanding of the market value and demand for different types of domain names.

Lastly, it is important to conduct thorough research and due diligence before appraising a domain name. Factors such as trademark infringement, domain history, and potential legal issues can significantly impact the value of a domain. Therefore, it is crucial to use tools like the United States Patent and Trademark Office (USPTO) or domain history lookup services to ensure that the domain you are appraising is free of any potential complications.

By utilizing these tools and resources, you can become a more proficient domain appraiser. Whether you choose to specialize in domain flipping, domain investing, or any other domain-related niche, having a solid understanding of domain appraisal will give you a competitive edge in the industry. So, take advantage of these tools, stay informed, and make wise appraisal decisions to maximize your potential for success in the world of domain flipping.

Providing Accurate Appraisals to Buyers and Sellers

When it comes to the world of domain flipping, one of the most important aspects is accurately appraising domain names. Whether you are a buyer or a seller, understanding the true value of a domain name is crucial for making informed decisions and maximizing profits. In this subchapter, we will explore the significance of providing accurate appraisals to buyers and sellers in the domain flipping industry.

For entrepreneurs, students, fresh graduates, young entrepreneurs, and even parents looking to delve into the world of domain flipping, understanding the value of domain names is essential. It can be the difference between making a profitable investment or losing money. Accurate appraisals help individuals identify high-value domain names and negotiate deals that align with their goals.

For those interested in making money from domain names, accurate appraisals are the foundation of success. Whether you are involved in domain flipping, domain parking, domain brokerage, domain investing, domain development, or domain monetization, understanding the value of domain names is crucial. Accurate appraisals allow you to recognize undervalued domains, negotiate better prices, and maximize your returns.

Additionally, for those offering domain registration services or domain consulting, accurate appraisals are vital for establishing trust and credibility with clients. By providing accurate assessments of domain values, you can offer expert advice and guidance on domain name strategies and help clients make informed decisions about their investments.

Moreover, accurate appraisals play a significant role in domain auctions. Participating in online domain auctions can be a profitable venture, but it requires a deep understanding of domain values. Accurate appraisals enable you to identify valuable domains, bid strategically, and profit from buying and selling domain names in auctions.

In conclusion, providing accurate appraisals to buyers and sellers is a fundamental skill in the domain flipping industry. It is essential for entrepreneurs, students, fresh graduates, young entrepreneurs, and even parents looking to enter the world of domain flipping. Accurate appraisals help individuals make informed decisions, identify high-value domains, negotiate better deals, and ultimately maximize their profits. Whether you are involved in domain flipping, domain parking, domain brokerage, domain investing, domain development, domain monetization, domain registration services, domain consulting, or domain auctions, accurate appraisals are the key to success in the domain flipping business.

Chapter 11: Domain Consulting: Expert Advice for Successful Domain Strategies

Becoming a Domain Consultant

In the world of digital entrepreneurship, domain flipping has emerged as a lucrative avenue for making money online. If you're an entrepreneur, student, fresh graduate, young entrepreneur, or even a parent looking for ways to generate income, becoming a domain consultant could be an exciting and profitable career option. This subchapter explores the various aspects of becoming a domain consultant and how it can benefit you in the domain flipping industry.

As a domain consultant, you have the expertise to offer valuable advice and guidance to individuals or businesses on domain name strategies. With your knowledge and experience, you can help clients make informed decisions regarding domain investing, domain development, domain monetization, domain registration services, and more.

One of the key benefits of becoming a domain consultant is the potential to earn a substantial income. By leveraging your expertise, you can charge consulting fees and provide services to clients who are willing to pay for your valuable insights. Furthermore, as the demand for domain consulting services continues to grow, you can expand your client base and establish yourself as a trusted authority in the industry.

Another advantage of being a domain consultant is the flexibility it offers. You can choose to work as a freelance consultant, providing services on a project basis or as an ongoing retainer. This flexibility allows you to manage your time effectively and work with clients from different industries or niches.

To become a successful domain consultant, it's essential to stay updated with the latest industry trends, tools, and techniques. This includes understanding the market value of domain names, staying informed about new domain extensions, and being aware of emerging opportunities in the domain flipping industry.

Networking and building relationships with domain investors, brokers, and other professionals in the industry can also enhance your credibility as a domain consultant. Attending industry conferences, joining online forums, and actively participating in domain auctions can help you expand your network and gain valuable insights into the market.

In conclusion, becoming a domain consultant is an excellent career choice for anyone interested in the domain flipping industry. With your expertise and guidance, you can help clients make informed decisions, increase their profits, and achieve success in the digital marketplace. So, if you're passionate about domain names and want to make a name for yourself in the domain flipping industry, consider becoming a domain consultant and unlock the potential for financial success and personal growth.

Offering Strategic Guidance to Clients

In the ever-evolving world of domain flipping, it is essential to have a solid understanding of the strategies that can help you succeed. Whether you are an entrepreneur, student, fresh graduate, young entrepreneur, or even a parent looking to explore new avenues of income generation, offering strategic guidance to clients is a crucial skill to develop.

The art of domain flipping encompasses various niches, each with its own set of opportunities and challenges. By providing expert advice and guidance, you can help individuals and businesses navigate through these niches and make informed decisions that maximize their profits. Let's explore some of the key areas where your strategic guidance can make a significant impact.

Domain investing is a popular strategy that involves building a portfolio of valuable domain names and earning income through their appreciation. As a strategic advisor, you can help clients identify valuable domain names, assess their potential for growth, and make informed investment decisions.

Domain development is another avenue where your expertise can be invaluable. By creating websites or online businesses on purchased domain names, clients can generate revenue through various monetization methods. Your guidance can help them identify the right niche, develop engaging content, and optimize their websites for maximum profitability.

Domain brokerage is yet another area where your strategic guidance can shine. Acting as a middleman, you can connect domain buyers and sellers, negotiating deals that benefit both parties. Your knowledge of market trends, valuations, and negotiation techniques can help clients secure profitable transactions and earn commissions.

Domain monetization and domain parking offer additional opportunities for generating income. By optimizing existing websites or blogs with valuable domain names and displaying ads on unused domain names, clients can earn passive income. Your guidance can help them maximize their monetization efforts and select the most lucrative advertising platforms.

Additionally, your expertise in domain registration services, domain appraisal, domain consulting, and domain auctions can further empower clients to make informed decisions and drive their domain flipping ventures to success.

In "Flip Your Fortune: The Art of Domain Flipping," you will learn the intricacies of offering strategic guidance to clients in the domain flipping industry. Through practical tips, case studies, and expert advice, this subchapter will equip you with the knowledge and skills needed to navigate the diverse niches within domain flipping and help clients achieve their financial goals.

No matter your background or experience level, this book will serve as a comprehensive guide to unlocking the potential of domain flipping and providing strategic guidance to clients. So, if you are ready to tap into the lucrative world of domain flipping and make a fortune, don't miss out on this invaluable resource.

Analyzing Market Trends and Opportunities

In the fast-paced world of domain flipping, staying ahead of market trends and identifying new opportunities is crucial to achieving success. By analyzing market trends, you can make informed decisions about which domain names to buy, sell, or develop, maximizing your chances of turning a profit. In this subchapter, we will explore various strategies for analyzing market trends and capitalizing on emerging opportunities in the domain flipping industry.

One of the first steps in analyzing market trends is to conduct thorough research. As an entrepreneur, student, fresh graduate, young entrepreneur, or even a parent looking to make some extra income, it is important to familiarize yourself with the current market conditions and the types of domain names that are in high demand. By monitoring industry news, attending conferences, and connecting with other domain flippers, you can gain valuable insights into the latest trends and potential profit-making opportunities.

Another effective strategy for analyzing market trends is to study historical sales data. By examining past sales records, you can identify patterns and trends that can help guide your decision-making process. Look for domains that have consistently sold for high prices or those that have experienced a sudden surge in demand. This information can provide valuable clues about where the market is heading and which domains are likely to be in high demand in the future.

Furthermore, it is essential to keep a close eye on emerging technologies, industries, and trends. As new technologies and industries emerge, the demand for relevant domain names often follows suit. Stay updated on the latest tech advancements, popular trends, and emerging industries to identify potential domain flipping opportunities before they become mainstream. For example, the rise of cryptocurrency led to a surge in demand for domain names related to blockchain and digital currencies.

Additionally, leveraging social media and online communities can provide valuable insights into market trends. Engage with fellow domain flippers, entrepreneurs, and industry experts through forums, blogs, and social media groups. By actively participating in these communities, you can learn from others' experiences, gain insider knowledge, and stay updated on the latest market trends.

In conclusion, analyzing market trends and identifying new opportunities is a crucial aspect of successful domain flipping. By conducting thorough research, studying historical sales data, staying updated on emerging technologies and industries, and engaging with online communities, you can position yourself to make informed decisions and maximize your profits. Whether you choose to focus on domain flipping, domain parking, domain brokerage, or any other niche within the domain industry, staying ahead of market trends will give you a competitive edge and increase your chances of success.

Helping Clients Make Informed Decisions

In the world of domain flipping, making informed decisions is crucial to success. Whether you're an entrepreneur, student, fresh graduate, young entrepreneur, or even a parent looking to delve into the domain flipping niche, understanding the different aspects of this industry can greatly impact your profits. This subchapter will explore various ways you can assist your clients in making informed decisions to maximize their returns.

One of the first steps to helping clients make informed decisions is by educating them about the different avenues within the domain flipping niche. From making money from domain names to domain parking, brokerage, investing, development, monetization, registration services, appraisal, consulting, and even participating in domain auctions, the possibilities are vast. By explaining these options in detail, clients can choose the path that aligns best with their goals and resources.

Next, it's essential to guide clients on how to research and evaluate potential domain names. Teach them the art of conducting thorough market research to identify trending keywords, niche industries, and target audiences. This knowledge will enable them to make informed decisions when purchasing domain names that have a higher chance of attracting potential buyers or generating revenue through organic traffic.

Furthermore, explain the importance of domain appraisal and the value it brings to the table. By offering domain appraisal services, clients can accurately determine the worth of their domain names, thus avoiding overpricing or underselling their assets. This knowledge empowers clients to negotiate better deals and make informed decisions when selling or buying domain names.

Another key aspect is providing guidance on monetizing existing websites or blogs with valuable domain names. Clients can optimize their online platforms for maximum profitability by incorporating effective marketing strategies, such as affiliate programs, sponsored content, or display ads. By understanding the potential revenue streams, clients can make informed decisions regarding the direction and growth of their online businesses.

Lastly, emphasize the importance of networking and staying updated with industry trends. Encourage clients to join domain flipping communities, attend conferences, and engage in online forums to connect with like-minded individuals. By keeping abreast of the latest news and developments, clients can make informed decisions based on market trends and buyer behavior.

In conclusion, helping clients make informed decisions in the domain flipping industry is a crucial aspect of your role as a domain flipping expert. By educating them on the various avenues, guiding them through research and evaluation processes, providing appraisal services, offering monetization strategies, and encouraging networking, you can empower your clients to make informed decisions that will ultimately lead to greater success and profitability in their domain flipping endeavors.

Chapter 12: Domain Auctions: Profiting from Online Domain Auctions

Participating in Online Domain Auctions

In the fast-paced digital world we live in today, domain flipping has emerged as a lucrative opportunity for entrepreneurs, students, fresh graduates, young entrepreneurs, and even parents. With the potential to make substantial profits, participating in online domain auctions is a strategy worth exploring.

Domain flipping involves buying and selling domain names for profit. It's a simple concept – you purchase a domain name at a low price and sell it at a higher price, pocketing the difference. However, success in domain flipping requires a keen eye for valuable domain names and a solid understanding of market trends.

One way to make money from domain names is through domain parking. By displaying ads on unused domain names, you can earn passive income. Domain brokerage is another avenue you can explore, acting as a middleman to connect domain buyers and sellers for a commission.

Domain investing involves building a portfolio of valuable domain names and earning income through their appreciation. It requires careful research and analysis to identify undervalued domains that have the potential for future growth.

For those with a knack for creativity and entrepreneurship, domain development offers an exciting opportunity. By creating websites or online businesses on purchased domain names, you can generate revenue through advertising, e-commerce, or other monetization methods.

Alternatively, if you already have existing websites or blogs with valuable domain names, domain monetization allows you to optimize and monetize them further to maximize your earnings.

Another way to profit from the domain industry is by offering domain registration services. By becoming a registrar, you can earn income through registration fees and provide valuable services to individuals and businesses looking to secure their online presence.

If you have a deep understanding of domain values, you can offer domain appraisal services. By providing expert opinions on the worth of domain names, you can assist buyers and sellers in making informed decisions.

For those with a wealth of knowledge and experience in the domain industry, domain consulting is a viable path. By offering expert advice and guidance on domain name strategies, you can assist individuals and businesses in navigating the complex world of domain flipping.

Lastly, participating in online domain auctions is a must for any domain flipper. These auctions provide a platform to buy and sell domain names, often at competitive prices. By honing your bidding skills and staying updated on market trends, you can make profitable transactions in these auctions.

In conclusion, participating in online domain auctions offers immense potential for entrepreneurs, students, fresh graduates, young entrepreneurs, and even parents. Whether you choose to focus on domain flipping, domain investing, domain development, or any other niche within the domain industry, the key to success lies in knowledge, research, and staying ahead of the curve. So, dive into the world of online domain auctions and unlock the opportunities waiting to be seized.

Strategies for Buying and Selling Domains at Auction

Chapter Overview:

In this subchapter, we will explore various strategies for buying and selling domains at auction. Whether you are an entrepreneur, student, fresh graduate, young entrepreneur, or a parent looking to explore new avenues of income, domain flipping can be a lucrative venture. We will delve into the niches of domain flipping, domain parking, domain brokerage, domain investing, domain development, domain monetization, domain registration services, domain appraisal, domain consulting, and domain auctions.

1. Domain Flipping:

Learn the art of buying low and selling high in the domain flipping niche. Discover effective strategies to identify undervalued domains, research their market potential, and sell them for a profit.

2. Domain Parking:

Explore the concept of earning money by displaying ads on unused domain names. Uncover strategies to optimize your parked domains for maximum revenue and ensure a steady stream of passive income.

3. Domain Brokerage:

Become a middleman and connect domain buyers and sellers for a commission. Learn negotiation tactics, marketing approaches, and networking strategies to excel in the domain brokerage business.

4. Domain Investing:

Build a valuable portfolio of domain names and earn income through their appreciation. Gain insights into domain valuation, market trends, and investment strategies to maximize your returns.

5. Domain Development:

Create websites or online businesses on purchased domain names to generate revenue. Discover strategies for content creation, search engine optimization, and monetization to make your developed domains profitable.

6. Domain Monetization:

Optimize and monetize existing websites or blogs with valuable domain names. Learn techniques to leverage traffic, affiliate marketing, and advertising to generate income from your domain assets.

7. Domain Registration Services:

Offer domain registration services and earn income through registration fees. Learn about domain registration platforms, marketing strategies, and customer retention techniques to establish a successful domain registration business.

8. Domain Appraisal:
Provide domain appraisal services to determine the value of domain names for buyers and sellers. Master the art of domain valuation and gain expertise in evaluating market demand, keywords, and brand potential.

9. Domain Consulting:
Offer expert advice and guidance on domain name strategies to individuals or businesses. Develop your consulting skills and become a trusted advisor in the domain industry.

10. Domain Auctions:
Participate in and profit from online domain auctions by buying and selling domain names. Discover effective bidding strategies, evaluate auction platforms, and learn how to spot valuable domains for auction success.

Conclusion:
With the strategies outlined in this subchapter, you can enter the exciting world of domain flipping, domain parking, domain brokerage, domain investing, and more. Whether you are looking for a side hustle or a full-time business opportunity, mastering these strategies will empower you to flip your fortune through the art of domain flipping.

Maximizing Profit Potential in Auctions

Auctions are a goldmine for entrepreneurs, students, fresh graduates, young entrepreneurs, and even parents looking to make some extra income. In the world of domain flipping, auctions can be a game-changer, providing the opportunity to buy and sell domain names for profit. In this subchapter, we will explore various strategies to maximize your profit potential in domain auctions.

One of the key ways to succeed in domain auctions is to have a clear understanding of your niche. Whether you are focused on making money from domain names, domain flipping, domain parking, domain brokerage, domain investing, or any other domain-related activity, knowing your niche will help you identify valuable domain names and make informed bidding decisions.

Research is the backbone of any successful auction strategy. Before participating in a domain auction, it is essential to conduct thorough research on the domain name's market value, potential buyers, and historical sales data. This information will enable you to set a realistic budget and avoid overpaying for a domain name that may not yield the desired returns.

Timing is everything in the auction world. Being aware of upcoming domain auctions and monitoring bidding activity can give you an edge over your competitors. By closely observing bidding patterns and identifying trends, you can strategically place your bids at the right time, increasing your chances of acquiring valuable domain names at a reasonable price.

Another effective strategy is to diversify your portfolio. Instead of focusing solely on buying and selling domain names, consider exploring other avenues such as domain development, domain monetization, domain registration services, or domain consulting. By diversifying your income streams, you can mitigate risks and maximize your profit potential.

Networking plays a vital role in the domain auction industry. Building relationships with fellow domain enthusiasts, brokers, and potential buyers can open doors to lucrative opportunities. Attending industry events, joining online forums, and leveraging social media platforms can help you connect with like-minded individuals, share insights, and stay updated on the latest trends and developments.

Lastly, don't be afraid to take calculated risks. Sometimes, bidding on a seemingly undervalued domain name or investing in a new niche can lead to significant profits. However, always remember to evaluate the risks and potential rewards before making any decisions.

In conclusion, maximizing profit potential in domain auctions requires a combination of research, strategy, timing, diversification, networking, and calculated risks. By following these guidelines and staying informed about the various niches within the domain industry, you can elevate your domain flipping game and turn it into a profitable venture. So, gear up, sharpen your bidding skills, and get ready to unlock the hidden potential of domain auctions.

Navigating Auction Platforms and Processes

In the fast-paced world of domain flipping, understanding how to navigate auction platforms and processes is essential for success. Whether you're an entrepreneur, student, fresh graduate, young entrepreneur, or even a parent looking to make some extra income, learning the ins and outs of auction platforms can be a game-changer in your domain flipping journey.

One of the most popular ways to make money from domain names is through domain auctions. These online marketplaces allow buyers and sellers to come together to buy and sell domain names. To participate in domain auctions, you need to create an account on these platforms and familiarize yourself with their bidding processes, rules, and fees.

When it comes to domain flipping, timing is crucial. Understanding how to identify and research valuable domain names that have the potential for high profits is essential. Auction platforms often provide tools and features that can help you analyze domain name metrics such as search volume, competition, and market trends. By utilizing these tools, you can make informed decisions and increase your chances of success.

It's important to note that while auction platforms offer a wide range of domain names, competition can be fierce. To stand out from the crowd, you need to develop effective bidding strategies. Set a budget, determine your maximum bid, and stick to it. Remember, the goal is to buy low and sell high, so don't get caught up in bidding wars that may eat into your potential profits.

Another aspect to consider is domain appraisal. Before participating in auctions, it's crucial to have a good understanding of a domain's value. Domain appraisal services can provide you with an estimate of a domain's worth based on factors such as its length, keywords, and market demand. This knowledge will help you make informed decisions about which domains to bid on and how much you should be willing to pay.

Lastly, once you've acquired valuable domain names through auctions, it's time to monetize them. This can be done through domain development, where you create websites or online businesses on these domains to generate revenue.

Alternatively, you can optimize and monetize existing websites or blogs by incorporating valuable domain names into their branding and content.

In conclusion, navigating auction platforms and processes is an essential skill for anyone looking to profit from domain flipping. By understanding how to research, bid strategically, appraise domain values, and monetize acquired domains, you can maximize your chances of success in this lucrative industry. So, dive into the world of domain auctions and flip your fortune today!

Chapter 13: Conclusion: Building Your Domain Flipping Empire

Recap of Key Strategies and Techniques

In this subchapter, we will recap the key strategies and techniques discussed throughout the book "Flip Your Fortune: The Art of Domain Flipping." Whether you are an entrepreneur, student, fresh graduate, young entrepreneur, or even a parent looking to explore new opportunities, the world of domain flipping offers various avenues to make money and generate income. Let's dive into the recap of the key strategies and techniques that can help you succeed in this dynamic field:

1. Make Money From Domain Names: Understand the value of domain names and how to leverage their potential to generate income.

2. Domain Flipping: Learn the art of buying and selling domain names for profit. Discover the strategies to identify undervalued domains and negotiate profitable deals.

3. Domain Parking: Explore the concept of earning money by displaying ads on unused domain names. Discover how to optimize parked domains for maximum revenue.

4. Domain Brokerage: Act as a middleman to connect domain buyers and sellers for a commission. Master the skills of negotiation and building relationships with potential clients.

5. Domain Investing: Build a portfolio of valuable domain names and earn income through their appreciation. Learn the techniques to identify high-potential domains and nurture them for future profits.

6. Domain Development: Create websites or online businesses on purchased domain names to generate revenue. Understand the essentials of web development and digital marketing to make your domains profitable.

7. Domain Monetization: Optimize and monetize existing websites or blogs with valuable domain names. Explore various strategies such as affiliate marketing, advertising, and sponsored content to maximize your earnings.

8. Domain Registration Services: Offer domain registration services and earn income through registration fees. Learn how to provide efficient and reliable services to attract customers.

9. Domain Appraisal: Provide domain appraisal services to determine the value of domain names for buyers and sellers. Master the techniques to evaluate the worth of a domain accurately.

10. Domain Consulting: Offer expert advice and guidance to individuals or businesses on domain name strategies. Develop your expertise and become a trusted consultant in the field.

11. Domain Auctions: Participate in and profit from online domain auctions by buying and selling domain names. Understand the bidding process and learn to identify valuable domains in auctions.

By understanding and implementing these strategies and techniques, you can unlock the potential of domain flipping and create a profitable venture. Whether you choose to focus on one niche or explore multiple avenues, the key lies in continuous learning, adaptability, and staying updated with the latest trends in the domain industry. Remember, success in domain flipping requires patience, persistence, and a keen eye for spotting opportunities.

Overcoming Challenges and Adapting to Market Changes

In the fast-paced world of domain flipping, it is crucial for entrepreneurs, students, fresh graduates, young entrepreneurs, and even parents to be able to overcome challenges and adapt to market changes. The art of domain flipping, as explored in "Flip Your Fortune: The Art of Domain Flipping," offers numerous opportunities to make money from domain names. However, it is not without its obstacles.

One of the key challenges faced by domain flippers is staying ahead of the ever-evolving market trends. The internet landscape is constantly changing, and what may be a hot domain name today may become outdated tomorrow. It is essential to keep a finger on the pulse of the industry, staying up-to-date with the latest trends and technologies to identify new opportunities.

Another challenge is competition. As more and more individuals enter the domain flipping business, the competition becomes fiercer. To stand out in this crowded market, it is essential to have a unique selling proposition. This could be specializing in a specific niche, offering personalized services, or leveraging your expertise to provide value-added services such as domain consulting or appraisal.

Moreover, market changes can also present challenges. For instance, search engine algorithms or advertising policies may change, affecting the monetization potential of domain names. In such situations, domain flippers need to be adaptable and flexible. They must be quick to adapt their strategies, exploring new avenues for generating income, such as domain development or registration services.

To overcome these challenges and adapt to market changes, it is crucial to develop a growth mindset. This involves embracing a continuous learning mindset, constantly seeking new knowledge and skills to stay relevant in the industry. Engaging in networking events, industry conferences, and online forums can help connect with like-minded individuals and stay informed about the latest developments.

Furthermore, building a diverse portfolio of domain names can act as a buffer against market volatility. By investing in a mix of different domain types, such as generic, brandable, or niche-specific domains, one can mitigate risks and ensure steady income streams.

In conclusion, the domain flipping industry offers numerous avenues to make money, but it is not without its challenges. Overcoming these challenges and adapting to market changes requires a proactive and adaptable mindset. By staying informed, building a diverse portfolio, and constantly learning and evolving, entrepreneurs, students, fresh graduates, young entrepreneurs, and even parents can thrive in the dynamic world of domain flipping.

Scaling and Growing Your Domain Flipping Business

In the world of online entrepreneurship, domain flipping has emerged as a lucrative business opportunity. Whether you are an entrepreneur, student, fresh graduate, young entrepreneur, or even a parent looking to make some extra income, domain flipping can be a great way to generate profits. This subchapter will guide you through the process of scaling and growing your domain flipping business, allowing you to maximize your earnings and achieve success in this niche.

To start, it is essential to understand the various niches within the domain flipping industry. Make Money From Domain Names, Domain flipping: Buying and selling domain names for profit, Domain parking: Earning money by displaying ads on unused domain names, Domain brokerage: Acting as a middleman to connect domain buyers and sellers for a commission, Domain investing: Building a portfolio of valuable domain names and earning income through their appreciation, Domain development: Creating websites or online businesses on purchased domain names to generate revenue, Domain monetization: Optimizing and monetizing existing websites or blogs with valuable domain names, Domain registration services: Offering domain registration services and earning income through registration fees, Domain appraisal: Providing domain appraisal services to determine the value of domain names for buyers and sellers, Domain consulting: Offering expert advice and guidance to individuals or businesses on domain name strategies, Domain auctions: Participating in and profiting from online domain auctions by buying and selling domain names.

Once you have identified your niche, it's time to focus on scaling your business. Start by expanding your network and building relationships within the domain flipping community. Attend industry conferences, join online forums, and connect with fellow domain flippers. By networking and collaborating with others, you can gain valuable insights, access new opportunities, and potentially collaborate on larger projects.

Additionally, consider diversifying your domain portfolio. Instead of relying solely on buying and selling individual domain names, explore other avenues such as domain development or domain investing. By creating websites or online businesses on purchased domain names, you can generate continuous revenue streams. Similarly, building a portfolio of valuable domain names and earning income through their appreciation can prove to be a long-term investment strategy.

Investing in automation tools and technology is also crucial for scaling your domain flipping business. These tools can help you streamline your operations, manage multiple domains efficiently, and identify profitable domain opportunities. By leveraging technology, you can save time, increase productivity, and ultimately grow your business.

Finally, never underestimate the power of continuous learning and education. Stay updated with industry trends, follow domain flipping blogs, and invest in courses or training programs. The domain flipping landscape is constantly evolving, and by staying informed, you can stay ahead of the competition and capitalize on emerging opportunities.

In conclusion, scaling and growing your domain flipping business requires a strategic approach. By identifying your niche, expanding your network, diversifying your portfolio, embracing technology, and staying informed, you can take your domain flipping business to new heights. With dedication, persistence, and a willingness to adapt, you can turn domain flipping into a profitable and sustainable venture.

Inspiring Success Stories in Domain Flipping

Domain flipping, the art of buying and selling domain names for profit, has emerged as a lucrative business opportunity for entrepreneurs, students, fresh graduates, young entrepreneurs, and even parents looking to make some extra income. In this subchapter, we will explore some inspiring success stories that exemplify the potential and possibilities of domain flipping, catering to the various niches within this domain industry.

One remarkable success story is that of Sarah, a fresh graduate who stumbled upon domain flipping while searching for ways to make money online. With minimal investment, she began buying domain names with potential value and listing them on popular domain auction platforms. Within a few months, Sarah sold her first domain for a significant profit, which motivated her to continue her journey in domain flipping. Today, she has built a six-figure income through her expertise in identifying undervalued domains and strategically selling them to interested buyers.

Another inspiring story is that of Michael, a seasoned entrepreneur who transitioned from traditional business ventures to the domain industry. Recognizing the potential in domain development, he started purchasing domains and building profitable websites on them. By monetizing these websites through advertising and affiliate marketing, Michael generated a passive income stream that surpassed his previous ventures. His success in domain development has enabled him to create a portfolio of valuable domains, further increasing his income through their appreciation.

Jennifer, a stay-at-home parent, found her niche in domain registration services. With her knowledge and passion for domain names, she started offering domain registration services to individuals and businesses. Through her exceptional customer service and competitive pricing, Jennifer quickly gained a loyal client base. Today, she runs a flourishing domain registration business, earning a steady income through registration fees and providing additional services like domain appraisal and consulting.

These success stories demonstrate the diverse opportunities within the domain flipping industry. Whether it's through domain brokerage, domain investment, domain monetization, or any other niche, individuals from all walks of life can tap into this lucrative market and achieve financial success.

If you are an entrepreneur, student, fresh graduate, young entrepreneur, or a parent looking to explore the various niches within the domain flipping industry, these inspiring stories prove that with dedication, knowledge, and a strategic approach, you too can flip your fortune and create a profitable business in domain flipping.

Appendix:

Glossary of Domain Flipping Terms

As you venture into the exciting world of domain flipping, it's important to familiarize yourself with the key terms and concepts that you'll encounter along the way. In this subchapter, we present a comprehensive glossary of domain flipping terms to help you navigate through this profitable industry.

1. Make Money From Domain Names: This niche focuses on various strategies and techniques to generate income by buying and selling domain names. It encompasses the art of identifying valuable domains, negotiating lucrative deals, and maximizing profits through strategic marketing and sales tactics.

2. Domain flipping: Buying and selling domain names for profit. This term refers to the process of acquiring domains at a lower price and selling them at a higher price to interested buyers. Successful domain flippers possess the ability to identify undervalued domains with potential and negotiate profitable resale deals.

3. Domain parking: Earning money by displaying ads on unused domain names. Domain parking involves monetizing idle domains by displaying relevant advertisements on them. Entrepreneurs can earn passive income through pay-per-click advertising or by redirecting traffic to other websites.

4. Domain brokerage: Acting as a middleman to connect domain buyers and sellers for a commission. Domain brokers facilitate the buying and selling process by assisting buyers and sellers in negotiating fair deals. They earn a commission based on the final sale price of the domain.

5. Domain investing: Building a portfolio of valuable domain names and earning income through their appreciation. Domain investors focus on acquiring premium domains with the potential for increased value over time. They monetize their portfolios through sales, leasing, or development.

6. Domain development: Creating websites or online businesses on purchased domain names to generate revenue. This strategy involves building websites or online businesses on valuable domains to attract traffic and generate income through various monetization methods such as advertising, affiliate marketing, or selling products/services.

7. Domain monetization: Optimizing and monetizing existing websites or blogs with valuable domain names. This approach involves maximizing the revenue potential of existing websites by leveraging the value of their domain names. It includes strategies like improving search engine optimization, increasing traffic, and implementing effective advertising techniques.

8. Domain registration services: Offering domain registration services and earning income through registration fees. Domain registration services allow individuals and businesses to secure and register domain names for their websites. Entrepreneurs can provide these services and earn income through registration fees charged to customers.

9. Domain appraisal: Providing domain appraisal services to determine the value of domain names for buyers and sellers. Domain appraisers evaluate the worth of a domain by considering factors such as domain length, keyword relevance, market demand, and historical sales data. This service helps buyers and sellers make informed decisions regarding domain pricing.

10. Domain consulting: Offering expert advice and guidance to individuals or businesses on domain name strategies. Domain consultants provide professional input on domain acquisition, portfolio management, and overall domain strategy. They assist clients in maximizing their domain investment potential and achieving their business goals.

11. Domain auctions: Participating in and profiting from online domain auctions by buying and selling domain names. Domain auctions provide a platform for buyers and sellers to trade domains. Entrepreneurs can participate in auctions to acquire valuable domains at competitive prices or sell their domains to the highest bidder.

By familiarizing yourself with these domain flipping terms, you'll be equipped with the knowledge needed to navigate the domain flipping industry successfully. Whether you're an entrepreneur, student, fresh graduate, young entrepreneur, or even a parent seeking to explore the world of domain flipping, understanding these terms will pave the way for your success in this lucrative field.

Useful Resources and Tools for Domain Flipping

Domain flipping, the art of buying and selling domain names for profit, has become a lucrative business in the digital age. Whether you are an entrepreneur, student, fresh graduate, young entrepreneur, or even a parent looking to make some extra income, domain flipping offers a range of opportunities to explore. To help you navigate this exciting field, here are some useful resources and tools that can enhance your domain flipping journey.

1. Domain marketplaces: Websites like Sedo, Flippa, and GoDaddy Auctions provide a platform for buying and selling domain names. These marketplaces offer a wide range of domain names, giving you access to potential investment opportunities and potential buyers.

2. Keyword research tools: To maximize your chances of success, it's important to select domain names with high search volume and commercial value. Tools like Google Keyword Planner, SEMrush, and Moz's Keyword Explorer can help you identify popular keywords and assess their potential profitability.

3. Domain valuation tools: Determining the value of a domain name is crucial for negotiating the right price. Resources like EstiBot, GoDaddy Domain Appraisals, and Sedo's domain valuation tool can provide estimated values based on factors such as domain length, keyword popularity, and historical sales data.

4. Website builders: If you plan to develop websites or online businesses on your purchased domain names, user-friendly website builders like WordPress, Wix, and Shopify can help you create professional and attractive websites without requiring extensive technical expertise.

5. SEO tools: Search engine optimization (SEO) plays a vital role in driving traffic and increasing the value of your domains. Tools such as Google Analytics, Ahrefs, and Moz can help you optimize your websites, monitor rankings, and analyze competitors to stay ahead in the game.

6. Domain brokerage services: Acting as a middleman to connect domain buyers and sellers can be a profitable venture. Platforms like SedoMLS and Afternic offer domain brokerage services, enabling you to earn a commission for successfully connecting buyers and sellers.

7. Online forums and communities: Joining domain flipping communities and forums, such as NamePros and DNForum, can provide valuable insights, networking opportunities, and potential buyers or sellers. Engaging with experienced domain flippers can help you learn from their expertise and stay updated on industry trends.

Remember, domain flipping encompasses various niches, including domain parking, domain investing, domain development, and more. By utilizing these resources and tools, you can enhance your domain flipping skills and increase your chances of success in this dynamic and profitable industry.

Recommended Reading for Further Knowledge

In the exciting world of domain flipping, there is always something new to learn and explore. Whether you are an entrepreneur, student, fresh graduate, young entrepreneur, or even a parent looking to expand your knowledge, there are several recommended books that can provide valuable insights and strategies to help you succeed in the various niches of domain flipping.

1. "Domain Flipping: Buying and Selling Domain Names for Profit" by Zach Booker - This comprehensive guide offers a step-by-step approach to finding, acquiring, and selling domain names for maximum profit. It covers essential topics such as market research, valuation techniques, negotiation strategies, and effective marketing tactics.

2. "The Domain Game: How People Get Rich From Internet Domain Names" by David Kesmodel - This book delves into the fascinating stories of individuals who have made fortunes through domain investing and flipping. It provides valuable lessons, case studies, and insider tips from industry experts, shedding light on the art of acquiring and monetizing valuable domain names.

3. "Domain Names: How to Choose and Protect a Great Name for Your Website" by Elihu Feustel - For those interested in domain development and monetization, this book offers practical guidance on selecting the right domain name, building a successful website or online business, and maximizing revenue through effective optimization and monetization strategies.

4. "The Domain Name Handbook: High Stakes and Strategies in Cyberspace" by Ellen Rony and Peter R. Rony - This comprehensive resource covers all aspects of the domain industry, including domain registration, brokerage, appraisal, consulting, and more. It provides valuable insights into the evolving landscape of domain names and offers expert advice on navigating this dynamic market.

5. "Sedo: The Ultimate Guide to Buying and Selling Domain Names" by Kathy Nielsen - This book focuses on the domain brokerage and auction aspects of domain flipping. It provides a comprehensive overview of Sedo, one of the largest domain marketplaces, and offers practical tips and strategies for successfully buying and selling domain names through their platform.

These recommended books offer a wealth of knowledge and guidance for anyone interested in the various niches of domain flipping. Whether you are looking to make money from domain names, engage in domain brokerage, build a domain portfolio, or explore other avenues within this industry, these resources will equip you with the necessary tools and insights to succeed. Happy reading and best of luck on your domain flipping journey!

Frequently Asked Questions about Domain Flipping

1. What is domain flipping?

Domain flipping refers to the practice of buying domain names at a low price and then selling them at a higher price for profit. It involves identifying valuable domain names, acquiring them, and reselling them to interested buyers.

2. How can I make money from domain names?

There are several ways to make money from domain names. You can engage in domain flipping, where you buy and sell domain names for profit. Alternatively, you can earn money through domain parking by displaying ads on unused domain names. Another option is domain monetization, where you optimize and monetize existing websites or blogs with valuable domain names.

3. Can domain flipping be a viable business opportunity?

Yes, domain flipping can be a lucrative business opportunity if done correctly. It requires research, knowledge of market trends, and an understanding of domain valuation. By identifying valuable domain names and effectively marketing them to potential buyers, you can generate significant income.

4. Do I need technical skills to start domain flipping?

While technical skills can be beneficial, they are not necessarily mandatory for domain flipping. Basic computer literacy and internet navigation skills are usually sufficient. However, having a good understanding of domain name trends and market demand can greatly enhance your chances of success.

5. How do I determine the value of a domain name?

There are various factors to consider when determining the value of a domain name. These include the length and memorability of the domain, the keywords within it, market demand for similar domains, and any existing website traffic or revenue associated with the domain. You can also seek the assistance of domain appraisal services to get a professional evaluation.

6. Can I make a full-time income from domain flipping?

Yes, many entrepreneurs have successfully turned domain flipping into a full-time income stream. However, it requires dedication, persistence, and continuous learning to stay ahead in this competitive market. Starting part-time and gradually scaling up your efforts can be a smart approach.

7. Are there any legal considerations when flipping domain names?

While domain flipping itself is legal, there are certain legal considerations to keep in mind. It is essential to respect trademark laws and avoid infringing on intellectual property rights. Additionally, it is advisable to familiarize yourself with the terms and conditions of domain marketplaces to ensure compliance.

In conclusion, domain flipping offers a range of opportunities for entrepreneurs, students, fresh graduates, young entrepreneurs, and even parents. Whether you choose to engage in domain flipping, domain parking, domain development, or any other domain-related business model, understanding the market, acquiring valuable domain names, and effectively marketing them are key to success in this field.